AbunDance

A Fulfilled Path to Success

AbunDance

A Fulfilled Path to Success

Oxana Lovich

Copyright © 2024 by Oxana Lovich

All rights reserved. No part of this book may be used or reproduced in any manner whatsoever without prior written consent of the author, except as provided by the United States of America copyright law.

Published by Best Seller Publishing®, St. Augustine, FL
Best Seller Publishing® is a registered trademark.
Printed in the United States of America.
ISBN: 978-1-962595-20-9

This publication is designed to provide accurate and authoritative information with regard to the subject matter covered. It is sold with the understanding that the publisher is not engaged in rendering legal, accounting, or other professional advice. If legal advice or other expert assistance is required, the services of a competent professional should be sought. The opinions expressed by the author in this book are not endorsed by Best Seller Publishing® and are the sole responsibility of the author rendering the opinion.

For more information, please write:
Best Seller Publishing®
1775 US-1 #1070
St. Augustine, FL 32084
or call 1 (626) 765-9750
Visit us online at: www.BestSellerPublishing.org

CONTENTS

Introduction 1

Part I: Build a Strong Foundation

Chapter 1: Beyond Surviving—How to Thrive 15
Chapter 2: Start Living a Prosperous Life 25
Chapter 3: Health Is Your Wealth 43

Part II: Master All Limitations

Chapter 4: Sexuality Is Sacred, Not Sinful 65
Chapter 5: Your Beliefs Create Your Reality 79
Chapter 6: Identifying and Removing Subconscious Beliefs ... 89

Part III: Achieve Personal Greatness

Chapter 7: Master Your Self-Image 107
Chapter 8: Develop Your Willpower 117
Chapter 9: Eliminate Fears from Your Life 127

Part IV: Awaken Love Within

Chapter 10: The Power of Self-Love 143
Chapter 11: Sacred Space of Your Heart 159
Chapter 12: Create a Fulfilling Relationship 167

Part V: Develop Leadership Qualities

Chapter 13: Master Communication Skills (Part 1) 189
Chapter 14: Master Communication Skills (Part 2) 199
Chapter 15: Your Words Have Power 211

Part VI: Strengthen Your Intuition

Chapter 16: Sensing Beyond the Senses 225
Chapter 17: Just Ask! 239
Chapter 18: Powerful Creations 255

Part VII: Awaken to Your Sacred Purpose

Chapter 19: The Power of Being Present 263
Chapter 20: Discover Your Life's Purpose 277
Chapter 21: Reaching the Sacred Apex 287

INTRODUCTION

"Become the alchemist of your destiny."

This is the book to read if you are looking for a personal transformation on a new level. Many of you who turn to spiritual resources are probably craving more advanced knowledge on how to manifest goals and create the life of your design. In this book, I aim to introduce you to a proven and highly effective course of action to bring about this desired transformation.

If you are willing to put in the necessary work, you will be able to not only realize a life of success but also fulfillment. As you awaken to a new level of awareness, your perception of life will change from one of limitation to one of limitless creation. You will be reborn into the powerful creator you were incarnated to be, and the intention behind everything you do will achieve its highest calling. That is when abundance, bliss, and success will reflect that inner foundation.

This book was inspired by my own journey, my own drive to overcome the darkness and turn it into victory, victory over the limited and powerless part of me. The tragic events in my childhood prompted me for many years to travel the path of personal transformation.

My Story

At the age of five, I lost the most important person in my life, my father, to a horrific yet unfortunately common illness: cancer. My father was everything to me, and even though I was very young, I still remember how my life lost significance and joy, knowing he was gone forever.

Then, at the age of twelve, tragedy would strike again as my mother also succumbed to cancer. At that point, I lost the desire to live as well. I became rebellious and self-centered, and I did so many terrifying things that even my relatives turned their backs on me.

In addition to rejection by my own family, I endured physical and mental abuse. To make this story short, by the time I was sixteen years old, I was alone on the streets with nowhere to go. The lifestyle that I entered into was not one I am proud of sharing, especially as I fully knew what I was involved in. I surrounded myself with people who were heavily into drugs and other self-destructive behavior. It seemed that this would be my life from that point on, one of misery and self-sabotage.

Fortunately, there must have been an invisible angel who was always there for me in a time of need, or at least that was how I felt. One day, I received an insight to move to a different city, and that is exactly what I did. I relocated from Saint Petersburg to Moscow. That is when my life took a different turn. I stopped living an unhealthy lifestyle, started studying acting, and became a professional ballroom dancer.

Personal Transformation

It was not until many years later, though, that I experienced glimpses of unconditional love and contentment as I discovered the path of spirituality. Those joyful moments gave me hope and motivation for getting through unending self-criticism and self-inflicted suffering.

For years I worked to heal an enormous emotional pain that was with me wherever I went. Sometimes it felt like there was no space for things to happen that were worse than what I'd already endured, but they did. Nevertheless, I continued searching for a way to heal myself. I have probably attended thousands of different workshops, all in efforts to attain inner transformation.

Sometimes it felt like I was moving one step forward then two steps backward. What I later realized was that, despite the fact that I was on the spiritual path, I was actually moving further and further away from my internal self.

The material world created illusionary ways for me to prove that I was enough—that is why I chose an acting career. Yet, no matter what I did to show the world that I was enough, I was feeling more and more empty inside.

Fortunately, those years of suffering led me to experience a spiritual awakening. That is when I was able to release the enormous amount of pain I had been carrying for so many years. That is also when I felt inspired to improve even more profoundly. And in the process of this enriching journey, I discovered a powerful system, 7 Strings of Harmony, which completely altered my life and continuously transforms everyone who studies it and applies its principles.

A Musical Instrument

My personal journey ultimately revealed to me that any individual's life is like a musical instrument. When one or more strings of that instrument are out of tune, the music no longer sounds harmonious. The same is true for your life.

When you concentrate solely on only a few areas of it while dismissing the others, you create roadblocks that impede your success and fulfillment as a whole. This does not mean you shouldn't prioritize certain areas, but rather you should create balance among all of them.

The main areas I am talking about in this book are based upon your energy centers, or chakras, which have been subjects of interest and practice since ancient times by the greatest spiritual leaders and their followers.

These areas are:

1. Health and Prosperity
2. Sexuality and Creativity
3. Confidence and Willpower
4. Love and Relationships
5. Communication Skills
6. Intuitive Abilities
7. Higher Consciousness

CREATING BALANCE

What I have noticed in my experience is that many people lack knowledge about how to lead the life of abundance and fulfillment which is, not only possible but also the most natural path you can take. What I mean is success in every area of life seems unattainable for some individuals.

For instance, I have met those who achieved great wealth yet were unable to feel enough and, as a result, deep inside, were not fully satisfied. I have encountered individuals who were able to create loving relationships yet found themselves struggling to make ends meet. For that reason, they had limited opportunities and resources to spend quality time with each other. I have also met highly spiritual people who spent all their energy seeking enlightenment until they had no home to comfort them and poor health conditions that prevented them from feeling serene.

Now, it is worth pointing out that there is nothing wrong with being highly prosperous or spiritual, or searching for a fulfilling relationship. But one must understand that, without balancing all seven areas of life, the quality of each one of them is diminished.

On the contrary, when you create equilibrium and fulfillment in all areas, a natural state of happiness, abundance, and contentment begins governing your life. In this book, I will endeavor to show you how to achieve this new way of experiencing life. Let me introduce you to the seven steps to fulfilled success.

Seven Steps to Mastery

I would like to show you how to begin living an extraordinary life. I would like to introduce you to a highly effective way to bring into reality whatever you aspire to, through balancing and creating improvement in all seven areas of life. I will demonstrate to you how attention and inspired actions toward enhancement of the seven facets of your being will awaken your natural manifesting potential.

This process can be applied for attainment of any of your goals. In this chapter I will give you a hypothetical example of the steps needed to achieve financial success and how the seven areas will contribute to the enjoyable achievement of the goal. Let me show you the plan:

Health and Prosperity

In order to achieve success in any endeavor, you should expand your knowledge and awareness of the area of health and prosperity. You begin this path by discovering your life's purpose and unique gifts you can share with the world. Afterward, you shall define a goal and believe you can accomplish it.

Consciousness of prosperity is the key to attracting material wealth. If you do not believe that affluence is possible, you can study the most profound techniques, only to find yourself in the ocean of lack. Formulating a compelling action plan and mastering the tactics of modern-day success creation is another crucial step.

Rewiring your brain by becoming a person who is successful is important in order to energetically align with the desired outcome. Learning to manifest while engaging your heart is a highly effective skill which will not only accelerate the process but will also make it much more enjoyable.

Moreover, without vigorous health and wellness, you may create success, yet you will walk a prolonged path without vital energy and motivation; that is why these sub-areas are so closely interconnected.

Sexuality and Creativity

On your journey to success, it is essential to strengthen the area of sexuality because sexual energy is the energy of creation, and not only of a physical child but also of business ideas. It is probably one of the most vital energy sources to help you awaken creative ideas in order to effortlessly manifest your goals. A favorite quote of mine from highly influential American self-help author Napoleon Hill explains it powerfully: "Sexual energy is the creative energy of all creative geniuses."

Your beliefs create your reality, and just like sexual creative energy, are your pathway to inspired creativity, bliss, perfect health, and wealth. Without transforming limiting beliefs, it will be challenging to create a successful life while setting the direction for your actions and decisions.

Introduction

Confidence and Willpower

The next essential area you should concentrate on is your confidence and willpower. Self-confidence plays a vital role in achieving a successful life, as being confident means becoming unstoppable in any endeavor.

Furthermore, developing willpower leads to manifesting your goals more efficiently and productively, enabling you to build a strong and powerful personality, which is your doorway to limitless achievement.

Love and Relationships

The area of love and relationships is another vital area. Falling in love with yourself will result in you becoming a person who radiates positive frequencies. Love is among the highest vibrational emotions, which not only makes you a much happier person but also helps you in attracting more people who want to work with you. In this modern, fast-paced world, you frequently get hired and create stable business relationships not only through talent and skills but also due to your personality.

Also, when you love yourself, you eliminate drama and conflicts from your life. In doing this, you have so much more energy to spend on achieving your goals. By mastering self-love, you truly master all your relationships, which are mirrors of your inner state. And the quality of your relationships defines your state of being, which is an essential factor in manifesting success.

Communication Skills

Another crucial area to explore is communication skills, which are essential for opening up doors of opportunities. Success in any field becomes so much easier when you learn how to articulate clearly and effectively. From here, you can begin building meaningful connections.

When you learn the power of your voice, you can transform the lives of others and influence profound changes in the world, which should be the foundation of any lasting achievement. Moreover, being aware of the power of your spoken word will assist you to speak your success into existence.

Intuitive Abilities

Intuition is your way to inner knowledge; without that, it is so much easier to fail. It is not a coincidence that one of the world`s greatest geniuses, Albert Einstein, would spend hours in the bathtub connecting with his intuition, pondering life and calculations, among many other ideas.

Your intuition is your pathway to being in the right place at the right time. It is your best guide to choosing the right material to work on, making deals with people who will bring about the most positive influence in your life, even as far as helping you build business relationships. Dismissing your intuition can frequently lead to making damaging mistakes that may slow down your progress and negatively impede your growth.

Higher Consciousness

The final area of life is your ability to be present and live life in a state of higher consciousness. When you learn how to be present, you learn to appreciate your success, thus inviting more of it into your life.

That is when you lose attachment to the final outcome, and it stops being a source of challenge and stress. At that point, the journey itself becomes the source of pure bliss, and you begin experiencing life from elevated awareness.

When you are truly present, your goals become more profound, and you cease expending your vital energy on hyperactive thoughts. Instead, you are filled with energy and motivation to share your gifts with the world and, as result, start living your purpose effortlessly and successfully.

THE PATH TO MASTERY

Can you see now how much simpler and more enjoyable it will be to create success though implementing the vital seven areas of life? And the best part is, I am confident that everyone who is willing to profoundly learn and apply the system of mastering seven areas of life, which I teach you about in this book, will attain astonishing results. Continuous study of these concepts will create a quantum leap in the achievement of your goals and will have a profound impact on your state of being.

A little bit about me: I have studied with and am certified by the world-renowned hypnotherapist Marisa Peer. I hold certificates in Rapid Transformational Therapy (RTT), Neuro-Linguistic Programming (NLP), Ericksonian Hypnotherapy, Reiki, Ho`oponopono, and the Silva Method, as well as graduating from the University of California, Berkeley.

In addition to academical methods of education, at one point in my life, I immersed myself in the teachings of Native American peoples to learn from generations of healers within their cultures. My own journey, together with years of practice and continuous learning, allowed me to create a profound transformation not only in my own life but also in many of my students.

This book is structured in the way that you are introduced to seven areas of life and given practical steps to help make profound shifts in each one of them. Before you continue reading, I highly recommend writing each of these seven areas on a piece of paper and giving them a score from 1 to 10. This is done to discover where you are at in each area in your life. To do this exercise ask yourself, "How do I rate the following area?"

1. Health and Prosperity?
2. Sexuality and Creativity?
3. Confidence and Willpower?
4. Love and Relationships?
5. Communication Skills?
6. Intuitive Abilities?
7. Higher Consciousness?

Upon completion of this exercise, you will discover the areas that you should focus on improving. If you determine, for example, that confidence and willpower is the weakest area, then you can study Part III of this book, "Achieve Personal Greatness," in more depth than the rest. It doesn't mean, though, that you should skip any parts or chapters in the book as all the concepts are closely interconnected.

I would also like to mention that within the book I included many real-life stories. To keep the privacy of those in the stories I chose fictitious names rather than their real names. I did this out of respect for the people in the stories, so that I keep their personal details private.

By the time you finish this book, you will embody a profound transformation. You will understand how connected these areas are and see an immense improvement in the quality of your life.

Furthermore, if you commit to the practices within the steps, you will be able to define and experience "the true success," which is fulfillment and abundance in every area of your life. From here, you will be on the path to becoming a new, more powerful, more successful, and more fulfilled YOU.

PART I
BUILD A STRONG FOUNDATION

CHAPTER 1

BEYOND SURVIVING— HOW TO THRIVE

> "Stop living from a place of limitation
> and learn to thrive instead."

We all want more out of life. And that's exactly the problem. *Wanting.*

You have probably heard that what you focus on expands, and the premise behind some spiritual theories is to concentrate your thoughts on what you want most. And yet, the word "want" actually means the state of not having.

It is indeed important to focus your mind on the desired outcomes, as well as quiet any doubts and negative, self-limiting beliefs. But thinking of your goals as something off in the vague, distant future, or as something outside yourself that you need to "attract" can have detrimental side effects. You are actually unknowingly giving energy to the *lack*.

Many manifestation guides will advise you to visualize the ideal future or outcomes, but do not always explain why this is important. It is not meant to be merely an exercise in daydreaming. It is actually intended to create a specific *feeling* within you. The feeling of *already* mastering your goals. Here. *Now*. In the present-moment, rather than off in some near future.

Feelings and emotions, you see, are the language that the quantum field understands—the signals that our bodies constantly transmit out into the energetic ether, and not abstract images or the often-fragmented thoughts which accompany them. It does us no good to keep visualizing a big house if we do not know what it will feel like to wake up in it. Or perhaps, more importantly, to wake up feeling like the sort of person who would live in a place like that.

Expand Your Consciousness

Now, when it comes to what you wish to manifest, many visions will at some point involve becoming more prosperous. It is important to realize that there`s nothing wrong with that at *all*—please do not be shy about visualizing a better future for yourself and the people you love.

Remember, the goal is to thrive, not merely survive. To survive means to just get by, make ends meet, settling for the bare minimum. To thrive, meanwhile, is not merely to sustain but rather to grow and evolve. So, dare to dream big.

You are neither "greedy" nor "selfish" for thinking this way. Simply through the process of living more abundantly, you will inevitably be able to contribute to bettering other lives as well. Plus, your elevated level of energy can impact the world in ways you may not yet fully realize. So, no need to play humble or small. Trust in the circle of life and support good causes whenever you are able.

Simply shifting your perspective and starting to think and feel big, especially when a current situation may not even provide a hope for a better future, is easier said than done. How do you truly shift your state from surviving to thriving? Begin to focus on what you are able to do with the prosperity (remember, present tense) instead of simply acquiring it.

In my experience, focusing on how you can better people and impact the world tends to open numerous opportunities and welcome serendipity into your life. Whereas thinking merely of the money itself often has the opposite effect as it may keep you in a consistent state of attachment, which in some cases may even chase money away.

An Altered State of Consciousness

How do you learn to feel the state of infinite possibilities? Let`s look at the example of the Native American rain dance. If you were to go in search of the right way to do it, you would find as many variations on the songs and dance steps as there are tribes. In other words, there is no one "right" way to perform it.

The songs and dances are simply designed to induce trance states, specific brainwave patterns that neurologists have now confirmed create an altered state of consciousness, which is exactly why mantras are also used in meditation in different corners of the globe.

What matters during the process is what is happening on the *inside* as the dancers perform the rain dance and enter into these states. They know what it feels like to have rain pelting their shoulders, their hair getting heavier from the wetness, or mud slipping in between their toes—even when dancing on hard, parched earth. In other words, they experience the rain fully as if it were already here.

Vision Book

A powerful way to master a new desired inner state is by creating a vision book, a notebook that contains photos of a new you and the desires you are about to manifest, which will form a new program, a new possibility in your subconscious mind.

You are not always aware of how much you truly believe in the manifestation of the desired dreams until you are able to imagine them. That is why envisioning your aspirations is the key to realizing them in your reality, and that is when the vision book becomes your greatest tool.

When I began my speaking career, I still experienced some challenges with English, since it is not my first language. I found a photo of a woman speaking in front of a very large audience, placed it in my vision book, and looked at it daily.

At first it was hard to imagine I could be in the same position due to the challenges of the language barrier. The more I looked and vigorously experienced the possibility, however, the faster the confidence was built within me. And in just a few years, I myself was a speaker at multiple large events.

I recommend the vision book because you can have it with you anywhere you are—at work, in the car, on a plane, or on vacation. The notebook itself also becomes a *reminder* to perform this powerful practice, especially when you choose a bright, beautiful cover and place it where you can continually see it.

When you are looking at those images, feel the desired outcome in your heart and engage your body until you feel powerful emotions. That is when you will begin noticing increased motivation and miraculous synchronicities.

In other words, once you embody the new powerful image of you and start living as if you are that version, it will be manifested in your reality. What I have noticed while working with many successful individuals is that those who are considered to be lucky are the ones who consciously or unconsciously already live their desired goals in the present-moment, feeling excited and motivated. One thing to remember is that your vision book will produce much greater results when you are fully connected with your soul`s purpose and willing to take inspired actions.

Re-wiring the Brain

Did you know that quantum physics seems to be making new discoveries almost daily that back up the importance of having a positive mindset? For instance, the emerging science of neuroplasticity implies that the thoughts you think the most over time become even easier to think and occur more often as they develop new particular neural pathways. So, you are "quite literally" re-wiring your brain for success or failure daily.

If you keep telling yourself over and over that you can do something, pretty soon you will be able to do it. If you additionally incorporate a feeling of what it feels like to have already done it, then eventually you will be filled with enthusiasm and valuable insights that will lead to the manifestation of your desire.

Athletes and peak performers have used similar techniques for decades and with measurable results—and I am not talking about just in mood and mindset but in actual physical performance. A well-known case is that of competitive swimmer Mark Spitz, who underwent hypnosis and guided visualization prior to the 1972 Olympics. He not only won seven gold medals but also set a new world record with each one of them.

No one would be able to come close to Spitz`s accomplishment until Michael Phelps won eight gold medals at the 2008 Olympics, nearly 40 years later. Phelps, who went on to win an unbelievable twenty-three medals in all, also refers to what he calls "the mental video of the perfect race," which he replayed in his head each and every night before going to bed, and again each morning before getting into the water.

Today, many pro athletes, celebrity entertainers, corporate CEOs, and other successful people include meditation and visualization in their daily practice because of its effectiveness.

ABRACADABRA

Have you ever heard the word "Abracadabra"? Its meaning reveals the power of spoken words. Abracadabra, the conjuring phrase spoken by so many magicians when casting a spell, is actually an ancient Aramaic word that means, "As I speak, so I create." This gives you some idea of how potent affirmations can be, especially when they become a regular part of your day.

For this reason, start your day by reminding yourself how powerful you are. Recite to yourself what you truly are capable of creating. Cristiano Ronaldo, a famous football player, for example, tells himself and the world that he is the best at what he does, and the results that he creates continue proving that statement.

Now, speaking affirmations is one thing, but it is additionally beneficial to write them out, look at them, and feel them—in this way, you are engaging even more of your senses by simultaneously speaking, seeing, feeling, and hearing the positive words and intentions.

Just like the visualizations, your affirmations should also be present-tense statements, starting with "I am" rather than with "I will." The more often you practice them, the faster you`ll realize your new reality, so be sure to treat this time as a sacred ritual and a fun celebration, rather than a chore.

Unconscious Messages

This practice is far more important than you may realize because on a typical day, you are confronted with *hundreds of* negative messages compared to an average of only a few positive, reinforcing ones; it all depends on the environment with which you surround yourself. You may not consciously even register when you are exposed to them throughout the day, but your subconscious remembers everything.

For example, a small newspaper lying next to you on the train that portrays any sort of negative or fearful messages still reinforces a self-limiting mindset underneath the surface. Additionally, it has an accumulative effect. Therefore, part of the role of positive affirmations is to counter this effect and, as a result, support you in creating more favorable experiences.

Have you ever considered that almost all of society's laws center on somehow being wronged and what the resulting financial compensation should be? It feels a bit like a collective mindset is more frequently predisposed toward negative outcomes. Understand that what you surround yourself with the majority of the time may become your present at some future time.

And if society already has a predisposed bias to expect the negative and you wish to avoid needless struggle and conflict, then you must constantly be countering that influence with your own positive thoughts and feelings. In other words, you need to take back control and start living your life by intent and design, rather than by default.

Where are the laws dictating how to react if a random stranger suddenly shows up at your door with a bunch of colorful balloons? Some might think you a little odd for living life with such an expectation, yet when did doom and gloom become the accepted normal?

Here's a thought: do you hesitate to have positive expectations because they seldom happen, or do they perhaps happen less often than they should *because* of low societal expectations? The beautiful thing is *you* get to decide for yourself what your own normal is going to be from now on.

Your Inner Power

Things tend to work for you to the extent that you *believe* that they will. Again, it is easier to say than do, because you may not yet realize the influence of deeply rooted subconscious beliefs, a concept that I will introduce to you in the next chapters.

What I would like you to understand at this moment is that when you first start pursuing your dreams, you build the foundation for them in both your energetic and physical world. Despite the fact you may already feel and see those dreams in your imagination, it takes some time to strengthen them in an energetic form for them to start materializing in a physical one. That is why creating consistency in visualization and affirmation practices plays a vital role.

I also believe that the word "attract," just like the word "want," which I talked about at the beginning of the chapter, may not even be the correct one, for it still implies that whatever you desire is somehow separate from you. It never truly is once your perception is altered. Remember the little boy in the first Matrix film? "It is not the spoon that bends, it is only yourself."

A Step Ahead

Another powerful thing to know when you make a conscious decision to thrive is to go a few steps ahead in materializing your dreams. Let's say you are in the process of manifesting a prosperous career. What is the actual purpose? Is it to travel and explore the world? Is it to leave a positive impact? Is it to provide the best education for your children?

When you know the answers, start experiencing those visions in your imagination, and you will rarely lack any motivation. This way, you will not only build a powerful foundation for your goal but also gain clarity for its higher purpose. And always remember that your objectives have so many more chances to be realized when you are willing to put the necessary work toward them.

Gratitude

Gratitude is one of the most powerful feelings when it comes to making manifestation work for you. I know you may say, I have heard that so many times." But do you actually practice it? Many individuals are aware of the simple habits that should be incorporated into their lives on a daily basis but do not always implement them. Otherwise, self-help books would probably cease to exist as they are not only educational tools but also powerful reminders.

When I realized the importance of gratitude, I began practicing it daily. I also set reminders everywhere to create consistency: in my home, in my car, and on my telephone. Why? Because gratitude is the feeling of *already* having! It is not visualizing some distant, far-off future. It is now. It is not a hope or a wish. It is certainty. And certainty is one of the best cures for doubt and the fastest way to truly manifest anything.

Manifesting with Your Heart

Did you know that recent scientific studies have determined that your heart sends more information to the brain than the brain sends to the heart? Another important thing to know is that the heart actually has its own "brain."

What I have noticed in my own and my clients' experiences is that manifestation occurs more effortlessly when you engage your heart. In other words, it is much more powerful to *feel* the desired outcome as having happened already, because it simultaneously affects your emotions, body chemistry, and thoughts.

Contrarily, when you think of and experience the desired goal in the mind only, you have a harder time engaging your body and emotions, and the mind perceives everything through patterns built by previous occurrences. If in the past you went through failures, for example, the mind's perception may not allow you to experience a desired outcome to the fullest.

Additionally, even the most trained mind will contain negative messages. That is why even the richest people on earth have thoughts of lack and limitation. Therefore, learn to engage your heart in order to become an effortless manifestor.

In conclusion, in order to start thriving, imbue your visons with the essence of already being manifested. Find inspiring pictures of your goals being realized and place them in your new vision book. This, in turn, will lead you not only to see and experience your intentions a few steps ahead, but it will also awaken a deeper level of trust, motivation, and purpose.

Also become aware of the unconscious negative messages you may be surrounded by and replace them with positive affirmations. Lastly, manifest with your heart, and never forget to express gratitude for beginning to lead a remarkable life.

CHAPTER 2

START LIVING A PROSPEROUS LIFE

"Wealth and prosperity are manifested effortlessly when your mind, heart, and intuition are aligned."

Most people dream of a successful and prosperous life. Yet many individuals find themselves not living the life of their design. Why do you think that is? This planet, Earth, is a divine demonstration of a miracle. Look at the sky at night. We are surrounded by galaxies, stars, and planets. The day changes into the night, while the sun makes way for the moon. You are a miraculous creation, too, as you live on this earth. Just look at the intelligent work of your body. Recognize its divine synchronicity and its ability to heal itself. What I also believe is that everything on this earth has its purpose, and you were born with an incredible talent to create. That is why doubting your creative potential means doubting the universal act of creation.

Recognize that if you did not learn to design your reality, your capabilities would remain unused. You definitely didn't come here to struggle and experience limitations other than temporary ones that provide a way to grow, evolve, and realize your full potential.

Another essential aspect to understand is that limitations are not part of your identity but are instead learned filters that can also be easily transformed. When you have altered them, the principles of success you learn will be applied and manifested so much more effortlessly. Let's begin this life-changing journey.

Your Beliefs and Your Success

I once encountered someone who believed that a person's success level was preordained as though written in the stars. Do you think an individual with such a viewpoint will ever become successful? Only if they are convinced that *the stars chose them*. If they believe otherwise, they may never learn and experience their highest potential. I know another individual who believes she is always lucky. For some people, it is hard to believe in fairy tales, yet her life is filled with consistent miraculous stories of flowing success, love, and abundance.

Your beliefs are your foundation. A successful person is the one who believes they are destined for success and, therefore, feels inspired to take the right actions and steps toward their goals. An unsuccessful person is the one who doesn't believe in their own abilities to create or do something and, as a result, finds themself habitually procrastinating and failing.

An important example of how beliefs shape your reality is an anecdote about a Russian family. While Josiah, an only son, was still young, his father kept telling him, "You are the smartest boy, the most ambitious and successful." The boy grew up into the smartest, most ambitious, and successful man because that was the reality he knew.

The secret ingredient is found in this story. The boy learned powerful beliefs as a child. Early childhood is when you form your beliefs, which reside in the subconscious. Later in life, those beliefs become the projector of your reality. And the fastest, most effective way to shift them is by working directly with your *subconscious mind*, not your *conscious mind*.

Understand that success always begins with a desire to create or manifest something, and that strong intention can only bear fruit in the mind that believes in possibilities. That is why the journey of manifestation will require profound work on subconscious blocks. Otherwise, the knowledge that you gain will only be accepted by the conscious mind, which is responsible for a mere 5 percent of your decision making. That is clearly not enough for major changes to occur.

In the chapter "Your Beliefs Create Your Reality," you will learn how each person's subconscious beliefs play an important role in their destiny and acquire the knowledge on how to transform yours.

Personal Qualities and Success

There are certainly some common principles of acquiring success such as intention setting, action steps, belief in yourself, dedication, educational training, and different spiritual approaches. Nevertheless, in my experience, those principles do not always work in the same way for everybody, even for those who desire similar goals and apply similar techniques.

You could interview thousands of successful people, only to find out that they each possess unique ways. The secret of Oprah Winfrey's success, as she explained it, is the power of service and alignment with her own truth. For industrialist Henry Ford, it was the ability to integrate his own perspective with that of others.

For Richard Branson, his general warm-hearted nature, gratitude, as well as persistence are key drivers for personal and successful achievement.

While studying and observing many powerful and successful people, various character traits are noticeably common among them. These essential qualities include integrity, passion, self-discipline, authenticity, intuitive abilities, great communication skills, and knowledge of their higher purpose.

Developing these qualities will assist you greatly in bringing people into your life who believe in your products, in your services, or in your spoken word. The steps to success can be unique and different for everyone, while the qualities of truly successful people, in my opinion, can be very similar. Consequently, learn to develop those characteristics to accelerate your growth.

Realize that people will buy your products and services because they trust and admire YOU. Your customers should become loyal friends and family, rather than simply your financial base. For that reason, expand the value of your contribution, and as a result, you will provide service with higher intentionality.

The Intention of Your Success

There are different drives or reasons for success. One is an authentic desire to bring value, to change lives, and to influence positively. The other is simply to acquire more material objects, which easily leads toward a path of emptiness. There is nothing wrong with seeking prosperity, yet it is imperative that your inner state is not owned by money.

I believe that success can be fulfilling only when its purpose is deeper than mere financial satisfaction. We are all unconsciously connected, which is why others may frequently perceive your true intention.

On your path to success, however, it is important to create balance between giving and receiving. If you merely seek financial gratification, you may get lost in desperation, which in turn could shake your authority and the flow of abundance. Conversely, if you solely concentrate on bringing altruistic value to others without requiring appreciation, you run the risk of depleting your vital energy in the long run and negatively influencing the quality of the service you provide.

YOUR CORE MESSAGE

Before you decide to embark on becoming prosperous, ask yourself this—why do you desire success? While answering this simple yet profound question, you may not only realize the true reason behind your intention but also create what is known as a mission statement, a short summary of purpose and goals.

Let's take a look at a well-known example. Apple, Inc. employed a simple message, "Think different," meaning thinking differently from the norm. I believe this has enabled Apple to become one of the most successful technological firms today.

Such a statement implies a different way of experiencing technology. Before the first iPhone appeared on the market, people didn't realize that a little handheld device would, or even could, become not only an effective communication tool but also a way to open the world up to anybody and everybody.

With an iPhone, you can do all sorts of activities, from editing photos, making and uploading videos, talking to someone in close proximity or on the other side of the world to creating an article, or even writing a book. These and many other innovative functions became possible. And I have no doubt that Apple's core message helped influence those innovations and impacted the company to become a pioneering giant in its field.

ALL ANSWERS ARE WITHIN

How do you discover your compelling message? It all comes back to the expression: all the answers can be found within. Some people seem to be constantly searching and looking for insights somewhere outside themselves. That is why those individuals can be put in the category of general and non-original rather than special and unique.

What if you could always be at the right place at the right time, say the right thing, study the right information, and model the right action? Would that create success in every area of your life? It certainly would. But how do you know what the right choices for you are? This knowledge arises from connecting with your inner guidance and your subconscious mind.

At some point, everyone has probably felt a hunch to be somewhere, and after they followed it, the event had transformed their destiny. That is an example of being connected with intuition. And the lack of this essential connection leads to an insufficiency of synchronicity, luck, and success.

Yes, you can continue exploring various systems to achieve success, to improve yourself, and to learn other essential lessons. Those skills are certainly necessary for achieving results. Nonetheless, there are a plentitude of methods and strategies available, and unless you develop your intuitive talent—something I will help you do—you might find yourself spending years learning things that won't advance you on your journey.

THE ART OF ASKING QUESTIONS

To attune to your intuition, begin by asking questions and learn to receive the insights. Do not hold your expectations tightly as to how you will receive the information, since it may come in all kinds of unexpected ways. Just learn to trust in your own inner guidance.

I would like to introduce you to an example that will assist you greatly in this topic. I had a client who knew exactly what she wanted to accomplish, yet she felt frustrated as to which actions to take. A few years ago, Maria came to my office in Westwood, California. She desired to start an online sales business. However, there were many different directions that she could choose, and that is why she felt stuck.

I knew I could have given Maria my advice on how to become successful. Yet, how would I know if my approach was the right one for her? So instead, I educated Maria about her own inner wisdom, and how to tap into it. I encouraged her to have trust and confidence in the intuitive guidance. I taught Maria that asking questions was one of the most powerful techniques in order to become clear.

Realize that you are always connected to the infinite supply of information. Your intuition is a vast reservoir of knowledge, and while asking a clear question, you will receive the answer. Asking questions can be applied to any area of life about which you are uncertain.

The question you ask should be specific but not limiting. Imagine you hired a tailor to sew a wedding dress. How specific would you be? Probably extremely detailed because you know exactly what you want. Yet, please remain flexible in order to take advantage of unforeseen possibilities, because what you are asking for may be limiting an idea or a product. In other words, while leaving the space for possibilities, you can actually manifest something even better than you originally dreamed to accomplish.

In my time spent with Maria, we created a concise question and clarification of her desire such as "What actions do I need to take to easily generate the most abundance, success, and growth for my business in the foreseeable future? My ideal for success, abundance, and growth means my personal salary reaches

$8,000–$10,000 or more per month. I work with a great team of talented and passionate employees, who are productive and happy with their earnings and environment. I constantly receive a flow of new constructive ideas so that my monthly revenues are consistently growing, along with other unforeseen miraculous possibilities appearing on my path."

Notice how Maria did not ask to receive a million dollars in her first months. You can ask whatever you want, of course. Although, what you can actually imagine in the now will give rise to far greater results. Again, keep in mind that specificity in your questions does not limit the result as long as you leave a space for possibilities.

After making a request, it doesn't mean you should be sitting idly and waiting. Behind every success there is work. "I never dreamt about success. I worked for it," said Estée Lauder, an American businesswoman. And that's exactly what Maria did. She was studying the subject and creating a business plan for her goal.

In a few weeks, Maria encountered a seminar on digital marketing that she was intuitively drawn toward. After this lecture, she was led to many other powerful sources and people. Over the course of the next few months, she was not only more clear than ever about the plan, but also put her dream business into action. "It was the best decision of my life," Maria told me later. "The knowledge I gained at the seminars I was guided toward led me to a successful foundation for my company, which is now thriving. All of this happened because I trusted my inner guidance." In Part VI, "Strengthen Your Intuition," I will teach you how to connect more deeply with your sixth sense.

Competition Is Your Inspiration

We live in the world of competition, yet having competitors does not negatively affect the ones who have found their own unique way to inspire, sell, or create. Competition should be the source of your continuous improvement and enthusiasm for greatness, rather than a source of fear and negativity. The most powerful way to compete is to compete with yourself. Strive to become greater every day.

Discover Your Higher Purpose

I've noticed in my experience that conventional methods of acquiring success do not guarantee immediate accomplishment. And practices such as visualization, asserting affirmations, vision board creation, intention writing, and a great work ethic do not always produce instant results.

I have had some people tell me that no matter how much they visualized and put actions toward their goals, they didn't attract what they were aiming for. There are a variety of reasons those steps fail to work such as a lack of focus and desire, the amount of time and work spent on the goal, procrastination patterns, weak intention, and self-sabotaging beliefs.

Please understand that I am not attempting to diminish the power of visualization practices. In the chapter "Beyond Surviving—How to Thrive," I stress the importance of this highly effective technique. Yet, there is something I would like to introduce you to that may awaken you to a new truth and perhaps help you to understand the law of attraction on a deeper level.

According to the law of attraction, you attract what you desire and what you believe you have already received. Nevertheless, what if the manifestation of that desire is not what is best for you to have at this moment? What if you are not fully aligned with your life's purpose? What if realizing your goal will not currently serve your growth? What if you are not able to cope with what you manifest?

There are examples of successful people such as Meryl Streep, Cate Blanchett, Charlize Theron, and others, who had no idea how successful and famous they would become. Yet, because they were living their *true life's purpose* and working passionately on their craft, opportunities opened up for them. That is why, in order to become fulfilled and successful, it is essential to *discover* your *life's purpose*. It is only by following your calling that you can be truly content.

If you have not yet connected with your true purpose, asking questions is a very powerful way to do so. What you can ask is, "What kind of career would I choose if all my bills were paid, I was financially secure, and I had all the time in the world?" This will lead you to other questions such as "What is my life's purpose?" "What am I best at?" "How can I serve humanity?" "What did I come to this earth to do?" Additionally, notice what hobbies and activities you enjoy doing the most. Find out what sets your soul on fire. In the chapter "Discover Your Life's Purpose," I provide additional insights on how to begin living your purpose.

Now I would like to introduce you to my own story. I was very young at the time I moved to the United States from Russia, and despite the fact I was already on a spiritual path, I chose a career of being an actress. While pursuing that vocation, I was persistent and hardworking. Also, at any free moment, I would practice visualizations, affirmations, and gratitude. At that time, new self-improvement programs and seminars were a part of my lifestyle.

In the course of five years, I achieved some great results. Yet, it did not feel like the doors of opportunity were opening up for me, and a deep emptiness overtook my heart. At certain moments, I started questioning everything.

One summer, in search of answers, I went on vacation by myself. I decided to go to Yosemite as it seemed like a peaceful place to meditate and spend some time soul-searching. I took my little dog, Buddha, with me on this trip, and as soon as I arrived at Yosemite, he started gasping for breath, maybe from the elevation, maybe from the heat, or maybe from a six-hour drive.

What I later realized was that the reason for his difficulty in breathing was perhaps completely different. When Buddha started suffocating, I got so afraid that I ran with him to a restaurant close by to get some water to cool him down. In the restaurant, I met a woman, and we shared a conversation that led me to change my destination. After having spoken to her, I decided to travel to Mount Shasta, where, for the first time in my life, I experienced a profound spiritual awakening.

I later realized that my intuition guided me there. I felt lost at the time, so right before I left on the drive, I asked my inner guidance where I should go in order to find myself. And I was led toward this awakening, life-changing journey.

Before I went to Mount Shasta, I would call myself a highly materialistic person. All my friends were very prominent. In Mount Shasta, I met a poor and slightly dirty hippie, a musician, who invited me to visit a spiritual ceremony with him. When I first saw him, I kind of judged him, but my soul and intuition urged me to go, and that is when my life changed completely.

For my whole life until this moment, I had thought I knew everything about spirituality, yet I realized I knew nothing. This whole time, I was proving something to others and myself, and that is why I'd chosen an acting career. This whole time, I was not living as a divine expression of myself.

During this quest, I remember sitting on the earth and, for the first time, experiencing the aliveness and the interconnectedness of all beings. My heart was fully open at that time, and the amount of love I felt at that moment changed forever how I perceive the world and people. And that is when I discovered my true purpose, which is becoming a transformational coach, and it is also when so, so, so many doors of opportunities began opening for me.

Did I waste five years of my life pursuing acting, though? Certainly not. What I realized is that sometimes there are different stages of development preparing you for your life`s true purpose. If the dedicated work, my intention, and visualization practices worked, and I became a highly established actress, I knew I would not feel fulfilled, and I would give it up eventually. The acting career, nonetheless, had prepared me for my true calling, transformational coaching.

Every experience in your life is there to teach you and help you evolve. Every experience, even failure, can be the door to success and growth. Each experience is like a staircase that takes you closer and closer to the evolution of yourself. It is hard to see it in the present because you are not always aware of what this part of the journey is preparing you for.

If I went back to the past, I would not change my choice to act as I learned to understand people through the characters I played. I also acquired the knowledge of how all characters build their destiny through their belief system. Additionally, I gained an understanding of how to stop judging because I walked in the shoes of many broken characters.

I also believe that you are always supported by Higher Intelligence, God, or whatever else you name this power. It is the intelligence that created the world and created you and is a part of you as you are part of it.

That same intelligence is always there for you, to support and guide you, even if you don't feel or see it. This power is there to lead you to your life's purpose. And what truly leads to struggle and lack in any endeavor is your belief in separation from this miraculous force.

Love What You Do

Great things are created with time. No, it is not a belief; it is a fact. If you want to create a masterpiece, you must start with a very strong foundation and follow specific steps. And the only way to make this journey pleasant is to enjoy the process.

Morgan Freeman was once asked what he would be doing if he hadn't become a successful actor. He replied, "I would act." When you truly love what you do, you do it for fulfillment, rather than negative motivations. Freeman's response is also a great example of someone infinitely connected with their soul's or life's purpose.

Every career will require work if you want to become excellent at it. And if you don't love what you do, you will not put that extra hour in to be great at what you do. There is another famous quote from Steve Jobs, the American entrepreneur: "The only way to do great work is to love what you do." I would like to add to the quote: The only way you become successful is to love what you do and be attuned with your soul's purpose.

Life's Purpose

One of the reasons why some individuals create a life of lack and dissatisfaction is that they choose their work for financial comfort, status, or other societal reasons. I once encountered a person, a very talented artist, who, unfortunately, decided to pursue a law career—even though he disliked it—in the search of financial security. Within ten years, he felt unfulfilled and hated the job more and more as time went on. Additionally, the income he generated did not add any happiness or the sought-after stability. Realize that when the passion for what you do is missing, the productive results will be difficult to reach.

Another question may arise in regard to choosing your sphere of work: *How can I follow my purpose if my profession doesn't pay enough money?* There are all kinds of stereotypical beliefs that exist in this world, such as the one saying that people who are artists, actors, yoga instructors, musicians, and cooks often struggle financially.

While it is true that some professions bring in less money than others, there is always a way to succeed economically when you pursue your life's purpose. I strongly believe that living with the assumption that certain vocations are not profitable enough will create lack of success and abundance in that sphere.

Consequently, follow your heart while choosing your career, because truly any profession can be your greatest success if you believe in yourself and have passion for it. Realize that if you are following your soul's purpose and love what you do, you are already successful. You can become a leader and an influencer in any job when you do it with immense passion.

Ahead of the Game

The world and its economy are changing rapidly. The same level of thinking and actions that worked even a year ago may no longer be effective. The companies that achieve massive success in the modern world are the ones that are constantly renovating their products and services and creating new ways to market and sell.

Changes in the marketplace are inevitable, even massive ones such as those caused by the COVID-19 pandemic. Some companies went out of business, while others became more successful.

I have a friend who owns a yoga studio in Los Angeles. During the first days of the pandemic, he moved everything online and offered all the members of the studio a free month's access.

My friend was testing this new method and actually increased the revenue and was able to double and even triple the number of attendees. One technique he used was altering the advertising style to reach a larger audience. As a result, not only does my friend still have the yoga studio, which was reopened to the public, but his operations have now expanded in a way that has multiplied his income.

Marketing Genius

Some people are afraid of selling and charging for their services. If you find yourself in this category, realize that you are offering support, maybe even saving someone else's life, and in return receiving a gratuity.

Another important aspect to know is that the key for your service or product to be discovered is effective marketing strategy and advertising. This particular area is broad, and probably only the entire book can cover every detail. My advice in order to create your marketing message would be:

1. State the problem you solve and the solution you provide.
2. Explain how your service or product guarantees satisfaction.
3. State the time it will take for your clients to achieve those results.
4. Make it easy. The less struggle your prospects experience to get their results, the better your system or product is.
5. Describe your plan for solving a problem in greater detail.

Recognize that everyone chooses to invest in products or services that they trust. That is why, if you were in need of a doctor, for example, you would most certainly choose an expert in the field. Given you have adequate experience, do not be afraid to call yourself an expert and have total confidence in the services you provide. Do not be afraid that you are uncapable of creating something unique and valuable. The world is changing rapidly, just like the needs of consumers.

What you are contributing to the world may even be essentially the same as it has always been, but you and your uniqueness are suited to deliver it in the modern age. Decide that you can do it. Remember a famous quote of Confucius, a Chinese philosopher: "The man who says he can and the man who says he cannot are both correct."

Another important detail to know is that people love to invest in products or services that provide them with some guarantee. In my opinion, one of the reasons Amazon has become so successful is due to its excellent customer service. Consumers do not have to fight to get a refund for something they are not satisfied with.

Nevertheless, the number of dissatisfied customers and refunds will significantly decrease once the quality of your service reaches its highest potential. This way, you will also organically influence the growth of new business.

I will stress again that the most successful people are not the ones who are stealing the competition but the ones who create powerful connections and relationships with their clients by building trust and providing an exceptional service.

THE POWER OF NON-ATTACHMENT

In my experience with various entrepreneurs, I have noticed that those who focus solely on money are often the ones who suffer the most financial setbacks. Life is there for you to enjoy and experience abundance. That is why those who put all their energy into their finances may lose sight of that truth.

I have met some individuals who can't even enjoy their vacations. They are constantly checking their bank accounts to see how much they spent instead of allowing themselves to enjoy the capital they have created. Instead of taking the time to rest, recharge, and revitalize and, as a result, to receive powerful new ideas, they get stuck in fears about the future. The truth is that individuals who reside in a constant state of worry and concern actually manifest those outcomes.

The flow of money can be compared to the stock market. One month it can be higher, and another month it may be lower. Yet, when you trust and believe in its consistent flow, you welcome the current of abundance into your life.

On the contrary, when you constantly attempt to control everything, are afraid to spend what you earn and allow fears to govern your life, you manifest lack and limitations. *Remember, your destiny is shaped by your daily decisions. So, choose the path of prosperity and abundance.*

In conclusion, in order to start living a prosperous life, you should transform limiting beliefs, begin following your life's purpose, and discover the reason for your success. Connect with intuition, which will, in turn, guide you toward manifestation of your aspirations.

Discover your unique gifts, develop qualities of a truly successful person, and create a compelling marketing strategy so that you can bring value to other people's lives, and in return, you will be rewarded with prosperity and a secure reputation in your field. Lastly, it is essential to feel abundant, reduce any attachments you may have to money, and work passionately toward your dreams.

AbunDance

CHAPTER 3

HEALTH IS YOUR WEALTH

> "The first wealth is health."
> — Ralph Waldo Emerson

Health is the area of life that is often dismissed or downplayed, especially by young people whose existence thus far has been free of physical ailments. As a result, it is common for individuals to take their physical well-being for granted.

On my journey, I have met people who realized that health was their greatest gift only when they were facing terminal illness or some other serious challenge. Why wait until your body fails to realize that you are mortal? Instead, I urge you to invest your time in developing healthy habits that will sustain you.

Realize that when this important aspect of life is not at its optimal level, material possessions, relationships, and the manifestation of goals will have little significance. Fortunately, you can take complete control of the choices you make today, which will determine your outcomes.

Your Inner State

Did you know that your overall physical health is directly interconnected with the thoughts you think and the emotions you feel? According to the Mayo Clinic, "Positive thinking helps with stress management and can even improve your health."

The Mayo Clinic also discovers additional potential advantages of positive thinking, such as an increased life span, greater resistance to everything from depression to the common cold, better psychological and physical well-being, reduced risk of death from cardiovascular disease, and better coping skills during times of hardship.

In 1976, author Louise Hay wrote a landmark book titled *How to Heal Your Body*, in which she showed the direct connection between different emotions and the physical problems that a person may experience. For example, allergies are the symptom of denying your own power, while lower back pain comes from financial fears.

I do believe that your emotional state is one of the most important influences on your well-being. What I notice while observing my clients and my own self is that, while healthy diet and supplements are vital for your health, without emotional balance, they do not generate a 100 percent beneficial effect.

The Effects of Emotional State

Did you know that even the healthiest, most nutritious foods and supplements may not have positive effects when you are experiencing negative emotions? The reason for this is the intention or feeling behind the action, which works similarly to the placebo effect.

The placebo effect, which I mention multiple times in my book due to its power and effectiveness, is a treatment or a drug that works due to the belief of the patient rather than its properties. I believe it works by the law of frequencies. For example, the belief in recovery and wellness radiates positive frequencies, while the belief in failure emits lower ones.

In the same way, while thinking or feeling negatively, you are unknowingly broadcasting low vibrational frequencies and charging your surroundings with them. That is why even the healthiest food in the world, if consumed or prepared in a state of anger or other negative emotions, gets charged by that emotional state, lowering its positive and healing effects. In contrast, feeling love or other optimistic emotions charges food with high-vibrational frequencies, and that is when food, water, and supplements become medicinal.

Have you ever experienced a situation when a certain food made you sick or unwell? Maybe it happened because you were feeling negative emotions, or the cook was preparing the food in a pessimistic emotional state. A famous experiment with water may be the answer to it.

Dr. Masaru Emoto concluded that our thoughts, emotions, and intentions impact our physical realm. He demonstrated this with an experiment in which water was exposed to positive and negative messages.

Afterward, the water was frozen, and the crystals were examined under a microscope. The loving, compassionate, and benevolent intentions resulted in aesthetically pleasing physical molecular formations, making them not only healthy but also healing. In comparison, water that was exposed to fearful and discordant human intentions resulted in disconnected, disfigured, and "unpleasant" physical ice crystal formations, which may negatively affect those who consume it.

Your Body Is Your Temple

With this experiment in mind, it is very important to create a loving relationship with your body. Realize that your body, just like everything in the universe, is a living energy field; therefore, become aware of how you communicate and interact with it. If you constantly criticize your weight or appearance, just like with water affected by negative intentions, your body`s vitality gets depreciated. Alternatively, loving and supporting thoughts positively influence your well-being.

In addition, your body is your best health coach. No matter the trials and tribulations, when you create a sacred connection with your body, it will always guide you on the path toward perfect health and vitality. You do so by first acknowledging its aliveness and starting to treat it with love and care.

There are so many different supplements and superfoods that you can incorporate into your diet that the selection process can be daunting. That is when you should ask your body, "Which ones will benefit my well-being the most?" You soon will be guided to the right answer.

For example, if you eat certain food and feel heaviness, stomach pain, negative emotions, or lack of energy, then this type of food, even if it is considered to be the healthiest one, may not be beneficial for you. On the contrary, foods that boost your energy and elevate your well-being should be incorporated more often.

Listening to the body is an amazing way to improve your health, shape, and energy levels. Moreover, you can add even more benefits by doing some research. Creating a healthy diet attuned to your individual needs can be tricky. We are all completely different, and what works for one person does not always work for another. There are so many different directions you can go, and to make the right choice, my recommendation will be to also learn about your blood type.

BLOOD TYPES

There are four different types of blood: O, A, B, and AB. All of them suggest different diets.

1. Blood type O—the most beneficial meal plan is made up of high-protein foods such as meat, fish, and vegetables. It is recommended to limit grains, beans, and dairy.
2. Blood type A—the most beneficial diet is vegetarian, or meat-free. It is suggested to include lots of fruits and vegetables, beans, legumes, and whole grains.
3. Blood type B—the most beneficial meal plan includes lots of green vegetables, eggs, and some meat. Buckwheat, tomatoes, peanuts, corn, and wheat should be excluded.
4. Blood type AB—the most beneficial diet is primarily seafood with lots of green vegetables, tofu, and dairy. It is highly recommended to exclude alcohol, caffeine, and smoked or cured meats.

A broader description can be found online or in numerous nutritional books, and it is your choice whether you decide to follow those recommendations.

Some individuals have very strong beliefs on how being vegan, or vegetarian, or even pescatarian, is the healthiest way to live. According to the blood types listed above, you can see that any one option doesn't work for all people. Furthermore, the reason that some individuals often experience lack of energy and fatigue is deficiency of vital nutrition. That is why it is so very important to continue exploring dietary requirements.

Your Body Is Your Guide

Have you ever experienced a desire to eat something such as a watermelon or maybe some specific type of cheese? This is how your body communicates with you when you are lacking certain vitamins and minerals found in those foods.

Nonetheless, you should learn to distinguish the desire of the mind from the needs of the body. For instance, if you desire gummy bears or marshmallows, that craving most often occurs in the mind since your body doesn't require artificial sugar to function optimally. On the other hand, desiring salmon or hemp seeds can be a sign of the body's need of essential fatty acids such as omega-3 or omega-6.

Natural vs. Artificial

In the modern world, the food industry consists of both natural and artificial foods and products. Natural foods, which are a healthy choice, are the ones that you can grow such as various vegetables, fruits, grains, or nuts. Humanely raised meat, produced without the aid of antibiotics or other preservatives, and wild caught fish also belong to this food category.

Natural products are the ones you are able to make at home, including salads, sandwiches, fruit desserts, yogurt, soup, and other similar meals. Those products spoil and degrade in a few days, while synthetic, artificial, and GMO ones can last for decades without changing their form. These artificially produced foods are one of the root causes of many modern health challenges.

If you would like to know whether a product is natural or artificial, ask yourself one of the following questions. Can I make it at home? Can I grow it? Will it spoil in a few days? If the answers are negative, then, in most cases, the food is artificial.

For instance, refined sugar, gummy bears, corn syrup, and soda drinks are not usually made at home due to the use of chemical ingredients that are not readily available and the complexity of the process itself, and as a result, are not beneficial for your well-being.

Physical Food Addictions

Did you know that artificial and GMO foods are addictive not due to their taste and quality but rather due to the special additives they contain? One of the ways to stop your body from craving those foods is by cleaning them out of your system. In other words, the desire to eat artificial foods is sustained by the additives they contain.

It can be compared with a nicotine addiction. Once the substance is in your system, your body continues craving it. As soon as you eliminate it for a few days or more, the physical desire begins to subside.

Unfortunately, elimination of physical addiction is not the only step. Mental dependency on a certain unhealthy food influences unhealthy choices to a great extent. It happens since its foundation resides in the subconscious. That is why, until this pattern is transformed in the mind, many individuals feel powerless to conquer food addiction.

Mental Addictions

Transforming mental addictions begins with shifting associations. You may not be fully aware of how you are unconsciously programmed to be drawn to certain food choices.

There is a big difference between want and need. When your body wants something, it is often the outcome of a positive association with that product. The need, on the other hand, comes from the actual requirement for elimination of hunger or thirst or due to the deficiency of a specific nutrient.

How are unhealthy desires created? Let's say that as a child, or even as an adult, you were exposed to a Pepsi commercial. What is usually presented in it? The commercial probably portrays happy, thin, and energized people, all dancing and having fun while enjoying a can of this drink.

While an individual is watching it, without being fully aware, their subconscious is possibly creating a pattern in the mind that drinking Pepsi will make them happier, more energized, and maybe even slimmer. The only difference between a child and an adult is that the adult subconscious mind must watch something repeatedly to create a new association, whereas with the child, one time is sometimes all it takes to create a new pattern.

Imagine if in the same Pepsi commercial, you were shown what Pepsi really does to your body from the inside out. What if you could see overweight people who can hardly walk and whose faces look unhealthy, tired, and wrinkled. In this case, your association would be quite negative, and the desire for this drink may not even occur.

Childhood Associations

Whether the people closest to you during childhood exercise their power positively or negatively, they are able to influence you when forming eating habits and beliefs. Please do not hold a grudge against them for the negative influences since in most cases they do not do it purposefully. They do it because they are unaware of the impact it creates on your life.

A great example of this type of influence is a loving parent who gives their child candy as a reward for good behavior. What kind of associations do you think the youngster creates as a result? Most certainly, this will be: "Candy is my way to reward myself for good behavior."

An individual who learns this pattern as a child may find themselves experiencing constant cravings for sugary foods in times of celebration. It is okay if it happens once in a while. Yet the same pattern can also turn into an addiction to sweet foods, since reasons to celebrate can happen every day or even multiple times a day.

Parents who give candy to their child in times of suffering are another example. This youngster, as an adult, may now reach for sugary foods in stressful and turbulent situations as they perceive them as a way to soothe pain.

It is not only parents who create negative associations; media and television may impact those patterns as well. Let's talk about movies that portray characters who begin eating chips, ice cream, and all sorts of other unhealthy snacks to cope with a horrible breakup or a divorce. As a result of watching those types of motion pictures, an individual may unconsciously create an association that those types of food soothe pain or help cope with challenges.

Questioning Your Associations

Despite the fact that your emotional state is capable of positively influencing how often you eat, it is a lot harder to modify unhealthy, artificial, and GMO foods into high-vibrational ones. You only have so much energy each day; why not use it wisely? For that reason, it is essential to create healthy eating habits and, consequently, use your vital daily energy for more important tasks.

How can unhealthy food preferences be broken? Realize that it is never about losing your favorite snack; it is about transforming what you believe. Starting today, begin questioning your associations with certain products.

For example, let's say you love sweet food. Realize that your body needs only about 25–35 grams of sugar daily. Vegetables, fruits, and even products you may not consider sweet easily fulfill the daily quota. If you continually crave sugary snacks after satisfying the actual need, it is purely a mind addiction.

Transform Mind Addictions

Transmuting mind addictions begins with elimination of self-created illusions. If you perceive a marshmallow, for example, as being an emotional support or crutch, it is time to reveal its true identity. As I mentioned earlier, every time you believe that a certain product provides any emotional support, it may be because as a little child, every time you were upset, one of your parents gave you that type of food.

Now it is time to make more responsible choices. Shift the associations in your mind by giving the "favorite snack" a new name. For example, marshmallow can possibly be named "white deadly poison." What is important while choosing the name is that it creates something that provokes disgust or dislike.

In other words, associate an unhealthy product with pain. Write down the negative impacts it has on your health, beauty, and longevity. Find pictures that portray those outcomes (aging skin, a fatigued person, or cellulite), print them, and place them next to a picture of an unhealthy snack.

Keep those images in multiple, visible places. Look at them before going to sleep and first thing in the morning to create a new belief in the subconscious mind. Repeat this exercise for 21 days or more, and soon you will regain power over the harmful food choices.

Additionally, begin questioning the association with unhealthy food by asking a question: What does it really mean to me? Then check out the truthfulness of the answer. Is it a fact or a belief? Remember, the belief that certain foods add something to your well-being creates an unconscious habit of overconsumption. The good news is, once you are aware of this pattern, you are halfway free.

Healthy Substitutes

To change the cravings on an even more profound level, exchange detrimental food choices for healthy substitutes. That way, you are not giving anything up, but instead gaining health, vitality, and longevity. If you find yourself addicted to sugar, look online or in cookbooks to find healthy recipes for meals and snacks that are free of refined sugar and artificial ingredients. For example, you can bake an apple, sprinkle it with dried coconut or cacao, and then put raw Manuka honey or mashed dates on top.

You can find substitutes for every harmful product that you are drawn toward. Potato chips or fried potatoes are considered to be an unhealthy snack, yet you may crave them from time to time. Fortunately, potato chips or fried potato are mostly unhealthy due to the harmful oils, salt, and preservatives they are made with, as well as the way they are prepared.

There are so many brands in the marketplace that exclude preservatives and bake potato chips with organic Himalayan pink salt and heart-healthy oils. The chips that are cooked with these ingredients may not be considered superfoods, yet they become a healthy alternative.

My favorite substitute for chips is baked sweet potato with garlic, olive oil, and organic barbecue sauce. This dish is a great and healthy choice. It is high in beta-carotene, which is considered one of the best remedies to preserve the youth of your skin.

Some people are addicted to fast food such as hamburgers, French fries, or other similar meals. These foods can be found in fast-food chains and are not beneficial to your health because they are usually made with unnatural ingredients, unhealthy oils, and GMO products.

Fortunately, any burger can be healthy if you use organic whole grain bread or a gluten-free bun, fresh vegetables, grapeseed or avocado oil-based mayo or dressing, grass-fed meat, wild caught fish, free-range chicken, or vegetarian or vegan patties made from beans or grains. The process of cooking this delicious dish is very easy and quite enjoyable.

Addiction to sugary drinks such as sodas, sweet coffees, or energy drinks is also a common issue. To substitute soda, you can add lemon or other fruits and Manuka honey to carbonated water. If you wish to make a healthy delicious coffee drink, you can mix organic coffee, cocoa, raw honey, coconut milk, and even organic low-sugar whipped cream.

Matcha tea is an even better alternative to coffee. It is a very healthy, energizing, and exquisite elixir, especially when mixed with Manuka honey and coconut milk. If you are looking for a way to increase your energy naturally, use coconut water, matcha green tea, ginger, maca, lemons, or blended banana in your drink.

The great news is that once you begin incorporating fresh vegetables, fruits, healthy proteins, nuts, and grains, your body starts craving new healthy ingredients. It frequently happens that, when you begin consuming the highest quality food, you completely lose the desire to eat junk food.

You may also crave some unhealthy products only to realize after eating them that they are not really that satisfying and delicious. You may also not feel well after eating processed food and, therefore, create a new unpleasant association with it.

Overeating Is Not Your Natural State

Overeating, just like eating fast food, is another reason that some individuals struggle with poor health, excessive weight, and lack of energy. One of the causes of overeating is a lack of vital nutrition or mental addiction to unhealthy foods.

Eating artificial, GMO, and non-organic meats, vegetables, and white grains doesn't really provide the essential nutrients that your body needs, so you actually end up craving even more food. A good example of this is artificially flavored white flour products. They actually raise your insulin level, making you feel hungrier and unsatisfied.

Additionally, if you unconsciously believe that food adds something to your emotional well-being, you become addicted to continuously consuming it. As we already discussed, in order to shift this behavior, you should transform the underlying belief.

Your New Healthy Path

Eating artificial food and overeating can be compared to committing a slow suicide, because you constantly create small amounts of damage to your body. Over time, these habits create more profound harm that can result in a lack of energy or even a serious illness.

Why do it to yourself? It is so much more enjoyable to live life radiating beauty, health, and vitality. Just remember, you don't have to shift all negative patterns at once. Doing so would feel like a tremendous amount of work or pressure. Your brain is designed to prevent you from experiencing pain. Pressure and deprivation are linked to pain. That is why you may stop following your new healthy lifestyle.

Rather, start implementing good habits in small measurable amounts until the process becomes comfortable and enjoyable, and the new behavior turns into a new healthy way of living. To say it differently, begin incorporating some organic vegetables, a highly nutritious smoothie, or a vitamin-rich salad once or twice a day until you see that you are absolutely capable of making bigger changes.

There are so many healthy recipe books and YouTube videos available that you will never feel short of new ideas. If cooking doesn't feel like an option for you, become aware of the snacks or prepared foods you buy in the grocery store. Check the ingredients on the products and only buy those that are familiar to you. When there are too many ingredients that you don't know, they are most certainly artificial ones.

Please don't be harsh with yourself if sometimes you fall out of the pattern of healthy eating as being imperfect is a part of being human. In those moments, remind yourself of the principles of the placebo effect. If you believe that something will harm you, it will harm you. If you believe that something is beneficial for you, it will become so.

It doesn't mean, though, you should start making wrong choices consistently and believe they will benefit you. It just means that, if on occasion you consume unhealthy food, you should not believe that it will damage your system. Instead, enjoy every moment of your life and transform the frequencies of the food by happy emotions.

Vitamins and Supplements

What you also should know is that, even if you begin eating organic, healthy, and natural food, it does not mean you will always get enough vitamins and nutrients, since, in modern times, most of the soils around the world are depleted of nutrients. In addition, you never truly know how long the produce has been lying on the shelves.

Did you know that as soon as the vegetable or fruit is taken from the plant, it begins losing its nutritional value? That is why adding vitamins and supplements to your diet is a great way to create an optimally nutritious diet and greatly improve your wellness and vitality.

There are numerous vitamins, minerals, herbs, and powders you can incorporate in a daily routine. While choosing the right supplements, you can consult a professional nutritionist. Be aware of any health challenges you may have as some supplements may have negative effects.

Make sure you are buying the best quality products as some of them contain artificial ingredients and additives. I would like to introduce you to my list of supplements that transformed my health and wellness. I spread them out throughout the week or use my body as an intuitive guide while consuming them.

- *Panax ginseng* is an excellent supplement for your health and longevity because of its potent antioxidant content. It reduces inflammation, strengthens the immune system, and boosts energy levels.
- *Wild caught fish oil* is essential for the health of your brain, heart, mental health, memory, beautiful skin, hair, and bones.
- *Rhodiola rosea* is recommended for fighting fatigue, decreasing stress, and reducing depression. It strengthens the immune system and improves mental performance.
- *Ormus* enhances the immune system, slows the aging process, increases the rate of healing, and improves sleep and mental capacities.
- *L-Lysine* supports the immune system, promotes collagen growth, and helps the body to absorb nutrients essential for your health such as calcium, iron, and zinc.

- *Echinacea and goldenseal root* boost the immune system and support overall wellness.
- *Collagen* reverses skin aging and improves hair, nails, and skin quality. Additionally, it can help relieve joint pain and prevent bone loss.
- *Tongkat ali* stimulates libido, promotes muscle strength, reduces fatigue, and improves energy levels and athletic performance.
- *Goji berry* is one of the most nutritious supplements you can incorporate into your daily diet. Goji berries provide immune system support, promote healthy and radiant skin, improve mood, increase longevity, and protect against oxidants that are known to cause cancer.
- *Chia seeds* are an excellent source of omega-3 fatty acids, fiber, protein, and antioxidants. They assist in weight control, heart health, radiant skin, and healthy bones. Chia seeds may reduce inflammation and blood sugar levels.
- *Hemp seeds* are a great source of plant-based protein. They aid digestion, improve skin, protect the heart and brain, reduce inflammation, and support the immune system.
- *Spirulina* is a nutritious superfood that is high in protein and rich in vitamins and minerals. It improves gut health, lowers your cholesterol level, boosts metabolism, and supports mental health.
- *Reishi mushrooms* boost the immune system, improve energy levels, and may help control blood sugar and support the heart. Additionally, they possess anti-aging and anti-cancer properties and help detoxify your body.
- *Chaga mushrooms* are a nutritious superfood that is rich in vitamins and minerals. They slow down the aging process, support the immune system, may fight inflammation, lower blood sugar and cholesterol, as well as prevent cancer.

- *Lion's mane mushrooms* contain anti-cancer properties and are a great supplement for your immune system. They help in reducing inflammation, maintaining heart health, managing blood sugar, and supporting digestive health.
- *Acai berries* are rich in antioxidants that boost brain function, support the immune system, fight cancer cells, slow the aging process, and increase metabolism.
- *Flax seeds* are high in omega-3 fatty acids. They are great for the health of your brain, heart, skin, and digestion. Flax seeds improve cholesterol, may lower blood pressure, and even reduce the risk of cancer.
- *Pearl powder* contains amino acids and vital trace minerals. It boosts antioxidants and has anti-aging properties. It is highly recommended for glowing skin, an improved circulatory system, and a healthy liver.
- *Artichoke extract* supports liver detoxification and improves digestive health. It may help lower blood sugar and regulate blood pressure. Artichoke extract is loaded with nutrients, and that is why it is beneficial for general wellness.
- *Mullein leaf* assists in detoxifying and strengthening the lungs.
- *Burdock root* is rich in antioxidants. It assists with digestion, helps with skin disorders, and reduces chronic inflammation. Burdock root helps prevent some types of cancer and removes toxins from the blood.

Despite the effectiveness of the mentioned supplements, it must be stated that they are not intended to diagnose, treat, cure, or prevent any disease.

Health and Exercise

Another very effective way you can improve your health is by exercising regularly. Some individuals dismiss this essential practice completely for a variety of reasons such as lack of time, motivation, or desire.

Did you know that exercise not only improves your body image, but it also boosts the immune system, increases energy levels, prevents a variety of illnesses, and simply makes you feel happier? The good news is that regular exercise is simply a habit that you can learn to incorporate into a daily routine. If you are lacking motivation in this area, begin with small changes such as walking to go shopping instead of driving, or choosing to use the stairs instead of the elevator.

Many people associate exercising with hard work. It is another association that is created by the mind that is not based on reality. Exercise can become fun and entertaining if you assign a new meaning to it. Start affirming to yourself that physical activity is easy and pleasurable.

Discover activities that you enjoy such as riding a bicycle, dancing, hiking, swimming, martial arts, or any other ones. Exercise doesn't always mean going to the gym and sweating on the treadmill. Find something that becomes your hobby and source of enjoyment rather than a necessary activity.

If you think that there is not enough time for it, recognize that with regular exercise, you actually increase energy levels, productivity, and lengthen your life. Consequently, by exercising regularly, you will have more energy, efficient time, and motivation to complete the important tasks.

When you exercise, your mind releases endorphins in the brain, which leads to a greater feeling of happiness. While doing any cardio activities, your heart is pumping faster and breathing deepens, ensuring that both heart and lungs become stronger. Implementing a regular exercise regimen also improves the cardiovascular system and produces high levels of norepinephrine, leading to better concentration and reduced stress.

In conclusion, keep in mind that health is your wealth. You can never enjoy life to its fullest unless you are healthy and vibrant, both physically and mentally.

Your emotional state, connection with the body, healthy eating habits, and regular exercise are essential factors that influence your well-being. Learning about your blood type and beneficial supplements can assist you greatly on this journey, alongside the transformation of any negative associations and food addictions.

Recognize that it is far simpler to avoid losing something than to get it back, and that the choices you make today will continue to influence the results you experience tomorrow.

PART II
MASTER ALL LIMITATIONS

CHAPTER 4

SEXUALITY IS SACRED, NOT SINFUL

"Sexual energy is the sacred energy of creation, not a subject of shame or taboo."

It is no accident that the second chakra, the energy center responsible for how we experience sexuality, is called the sacral, coming from the word *sacred*, which means devoted to a deity or some religious purpose.

Some religions and traditions, however, have conditioned society to think of sex as something embarrassing or sinful, something to be talked about in shameful tones and reserved for darkened rooms. But quite the opposite is true. A new life, which is the most innocent form of existence, is created through this sacred act.

If you are coming from a traditional background and thinking about or discussing sexuality tends to trigger uncomfortable feelings, please consider that Higher Consciousness created this sacred ritual for a higher purpose: to create a new life-form, and that is actually how YOU were born. And this concept applies to almost every creature residing on this planet.

Please understand that if uncomfortable feelings arise while discussing this subject, they are most likely the result of some unconscious programming and misinterpretation of sexual energy.

Tantra—A Path to Awakening

Ancient spiritual traditions considered exploring sexual energy as the fastest path to awakening. Tantra is one such tradition. Rather than shunning sex, it embraces and even encourages it as an essential spiritual practice.

In fact, the word Tantra itself, in Sanskrit, simply means a technique or practice. But what is interesting about the Sanskrit language is that the individual syllables of a word itself have their own unique meaning, often emboldening you to consider a subject from several different perspectives.

The word *tan*, literally translated, means fabric or something woven together. Figuratively, it often represents the fabric of the universe and reality as a whole. The word *tra* means to transcend, or break free from. So, putting it all together, Tantra teaching is a way to transcend reality or break free from illusions and assumptions that, as a society, we have mistakenly taken as a reality.

Tantra not only teaches you to question everything and look beneath the surface, but it also introduces you to a new way to experience life on a deeper level and engage with it more fully, more consciously, and more deliberately. It is not merely a sexual practice; it is a way of living your entire life in a state of meditation, wonder, and appreciation.

The sacredness of this practice is closely related to the creative powerful force, sexual energy, which has the potential to illuminate the path for such visions as spiritual awakening, higher consciousness, success, the birth of a child, or any creative idea.

Acceptance of Your Sexuality

If you feel uncomfortable discussing the subject of intimacy in more depth, realize that in modern society, the perception of sexuality tends to be quite distorted and misunderstood due to the wrong information many individuals received as children and continue to be presented with from media and other sources.

I grew up in a family that taught me those misrepresented ways, and that is why I completely understand the unpleasant feelings the subject may stir. Realize, nonetheless, that where the most pain, shame, or other negative feelings reside is where your strength and power live as well. So instead of dismissing or running away from those uncomfortable triggers, discover the courage to delve deep within and transform those limitations. The next chapters on beliefs will assist you greatly in this process.

To shift your perception on sexuality, I would like to show it to you from a different angle. According to Wikipedia, the union of feminine and masculine, through sexuality, continues recreating life on our planet. For women who still have a hard time accepting their feminine sexual organs, I would like to add another sentence from the same source, which states: "The yoni is conceptualized as nature's gateway of all births . . . Yoni is a Sanskrit word that has been interpreted to literally mean the 'womb,' the 'source,' and the female organs of generation."

I hope this information creates a sense of pride in your ability to recreate this miraculous existence, and to assist in transmuting the emotions of shame and guilt connected with this subject.

Sexual Energy Is the Energy of Creation

Sexual energy is the most powerful process of creation, the creation of a new life-form, without which life would no longer continue. This powerful energy is capable of bringing to life not only a physical child but also the rise of creativity and realization of your heart's desires.

It is not a coincidence that one of the most famous books from the past on acquiring riches, *Think and Grow Rich* by Napoleon Hill (1939), has a whole chapter called "The Mystery of Sex Transmutation." It is a chapter on the importance of sex while manifesting your dreams. The quotation that follows gives the paramount idea:

> Sex desire is the most powerful of human desires. When driven by this desire, men develop keenness of imagination, courage, willpower, persistence, and creative ability unknown to them at other times. So strong and impelling is the desire for sexual contact that men freely run the risk of life and reputation to indulge it. When harnessed, and redirected along other lines, this motivating force maintains all of its attributes of keenness of imagination, courage, etc., which may be used as powerful creative forces in literature, art, or in any other profession or calling, including, of course, the accumulation of riches.

To state it differently, when you have a partner with whom you practice sacred sexuality, which is a spiritual connection that reaches beyond a physical one, you awaken an invincible force within to create and manifest your aspirations. You become a channel through which brilliant ideas come to fruition. Your energy level and motivation rise to their highest potential as you are governed by love and sacred desire.

What is essential to understand is that sexual energy is like all other energies: it can be used to either create or destroy. That is why I refer to the sexuality I am talking about as sacred. There is a big difference between sex that happens from mere lust and an instinctual desire vs. sex that merges two souls into one divine energy of transformation and awakened consciousness.

CREATIVE ENERGY

The connection between your sexuality and creativity may not be obvious at first. Remember though, sexual energy is the very energy that creates life in the first place. The connection runs even deeper than that as unmet or unexpressed sexual needs will often manifest themselves as creative blocks. And the same can also be true in reverse, for unexpressed creativity can often create issues with how well you connect sexually—both with yourself and another.

Before you delve deeper into the connection between sexuality and creativity, let's first bring some clarity on what creativity is in the first place. The most obvious things that probably spring to mind when you think of creativity might be art or music. But you don't need to be a painter, author, or a world-renowned performer in order to be creative.

Creativity is actually defined as the ability to transcend traditional ideas, rules, patterns, or relationships, and to create meaningful new ideas, methods, connections, or interpretations. Creativity is not only about the ability to imagine and dream but is also the very force that drives your progress—both as an individual and for society as a whole.

If you have a new business or product idea or come up with a way to improve an existing commodity, that is being creative. If you come up with a new or better way of doing something, that is being creative. If you decide to take a different route to work to be inspired by new scenery, that is creativity expressing itself through you.

As a matter of fact, if your vision for your life in any way expands beyond waking up every day just to go to work so that you can pay the bills, you are definitely creative. And since sexuality and creativity are closely interconnected, please don't dismiss this vital area, which is truly the bridge to your wildest aspirations.

Sexuality Is Magnetic

Have you noticed how much power and confidence people who are fully connected with their sexuality radiate? That is because by embracing sexual energy, you awaken the inner power as you embody the creative force within.

Some parents are afraid to speak to their growing children about the power of sexuality because they often perceive it as something uncomfortable and inappropriate. Adolescents subconsciously learn from their parents that there is something wrong with them; even one part of a youngster being viewed as unsuitable may lead to an undeniable feeling of incompleteness. This often results in a consistent need for validation, lack of inner power, and low self-esteem.

Therefore, learn to accept and embrace sexuality and, as a result, eliminate an unnecessary roadblock to developing a magnetic and successful personality, which is your birthright in the first place. Your life will not only become so much more enjoyable, but all your relationships will also reach a new level of depth and meaning.

Design Your Reality

Remember that you first create your reality on an energetic level, which is truly the invisible foundation you've built. That is why not everyone is aware of it. Realize that you also don't see radio waves, yet there is an invisible electronic current that creates a sound.

To manifest and create the life of your design is much easier and faster when you understand that you are much more than a physical body. You consist of energy, and when you learn how to use it correctly and with a pure motive, you accelerate the path toward fulfillment, happiness, and success.

The best way to manifest a desired outcome is to become conscious of how you build that invisible foundation, which, once it becomes stronger, begins materializing as the new reality. One of the very effective ways to do so is during sacred sex. That is exactly when the energy of creation and manifestation is at its highest peak. The fact that you don't see that invisible energy can make the process less powerful, as you may negatively influence it with feelings of mistrust and limiting perceptions. The more you are willing to feel and experience the invisible creative power within, contrarily, the faster you will exhibit the highest potential.

During a sexual sacred ritual, when one's heart is filled with love and a deep connection with one's partner, it is so much easier to shift from the busy mindful state into a pure present-moment awareness and unconditional love. These are a gateway toward formation of the magnetic connection between energetic and physical reality. That is the perfect time to feel and experience yourself as a person already obtaining the qualities the desired goals will provide.

For example, if you wish to manifest financial freedom, experience yourself in a state of affluence. These emotions will not only assist you in creating an effortless and miraculous journey toward your dreams, but they will also awaken a feeling of trust and a deeper connection with your inner guidance.

To say it differently, feel the core desires with your body and heart during a moment of the deepest connection with your partner. Again, when the inner monologues of the mind lose their significance and love sensations take over, you awaken the manifesting abilities. Afterward, take a breath of a new powerful you and recharge your cells with this energy and be open to accept those visions into your life.

Masculine and Feminine Polarities

Men are traditionally thought to be masculine and have yang energy. This energy is goal-oriented, focused, active, and strong. It is an upward-moving energy, which can help in achieving goals through strength and power. In contrast, women are traditionally thought to be feminine and have yin energy. This energy can be described as intuitive, empathetic, emotional, deeply caring, imaginative, and deeply affectionate.

Excessive masculine energy, or yang energy, can lead to many of the following challenges: aggression, excessive anger, inability to rest or reset, rapid heartbeat, excessive hunger, too much sweating, insomnia, emotional stress, overthinking, and even inflammation in the body. Much in the same way, having an overabundance of feminine energy can lead to being passive, slow, overly obedient, too soft, and pliable.

Imbalanced yin and yang energies can also create other challenges. For example, individuals who are excessively masculine tend to lack intuition, nurturing, and caring, while also being stubborn and inflexible. Those who are extremely feminine frequently lack concentration, confidence, ambition, and strength. And the best way to balance these qualities with each other is through sacred sex, during which you can imbue an opposite energy in you.

In order to master this practice, you need to reflect on whether you have more feminine or masculine energy. In modern times, for example, some women are more masculine, and some men are more feminine. Write down on a piece of paper your guiding personality traits.

Masculine traits, for example, might be proclivity and passion for competition such as sports and a strong desire to win. Feminine traits, for example, might be a cultivation of life such as gardening, cooking, and deep caring for an animal or a child. In relation to how each energy communicates: masculine is more direct and simpler, whereas feminine contains different layers of emotional complexity. Furthermore, you tend to attract a partner with opposite but similar balanced or imbalanced qualities, regardless of your gender.

During sacred sexuality, you are capable of creating a perfect equilibrium of these polarities. If you look at the typical picture depicting yin and yang, you will see that in the white part of the circle, there is a little black spot, while in the black part of the circle, there is a little white spot.

To express it differently, masculine polarity becomes more powerful when tempered with the softness of feminine energy. Feminine energy will achieve its highest potential when it includes a touch of the strength of masculinity.

Consequently, discern the qualities that you would like to improve which are the direct result of the polarity's imbalance. Afterward, write down the qualities of your partner that can have a great influence on you. The next time during lovemaking, take those qualities in with a deep breath or an imagined light.

The more you implement this practice, the faster you will give birth to new powerful qualities. The most important aspect is not to include the mind in this exercise. What I mean is, in general, a mind can be destructive to achieve transformation.

Let me explain it further: anytime you judge or describe any experience, you diminish its quality, because you are interpreting it in the mind rather than experiencing it in your heart. And only the mindless state, which is detachment from your own thoughts, will result in your truly experiencing and embedding the transformation that is the catalyst for a lasting change.

Pure Presence

Have you ever experienced a feeling that made you speechless? It is the goal of sacred sexuality. To get lost in one another in the sacred present-moment is to achieve a divine connection of oneness with each other and the source of life itself.

In other words, there is a big difference between imagining—an activity that takes place in the mind—and feeling the sensations with your body and heart. When you imagine something, it can be powerful. Although, it is not always attainable to get lost in it as the mind frequently has something else to add, like a doubt or a restless thought.

To the contrary, when you give yourself permission to feel every sensation, including deep love, you awaken all the cells in your body, which now can dance with one another, be filled with new energy, and ultimately reawaken, re-energize, and be revived. Once you reach this point, time and space start to lose significance and are replaced by present-moment awareness.

Realize that your overall success, happiness, and well-being in all aspects of your life are greatly enhanced by being in this state. Attaining present-moment awareness may require some dedication and consistent practice as it is mastered through repetition. And if your mind has been allowed to be the driver for, let's say, five, ten, or twenty or more years, it will require some time to embed a new positive pattern. In Chapter 19, "The Power of Being Present," I provide practical techniques to assist you further on this journey.

Your Partner's Needs

Additional advice I would like to give is, while practicing sacred sexuality, take your time. This is especially important if you are one of those individuals who tends to rush the process as a consequence of being taken over by the destination. I have heard complaints from quite a few men about how their wives do not satisfy their needs. They say that their significant others desire far less sex than they want.

The reason for this challenge is that visual imagery is the key in order for many men, especially the more masculine ones, to get sexually activated. In other words, just looking at the partner can create that feeling.

For many women, especially the most feminine, to be sexually awakened, they must trust their partner, connect emotionally, and feel loved and admired. If they don`t perceive these needs to be met, they may lose the desire for sexual pleasures altogether.

This doesn`t refer, nevertheless, to all men and women. I mentioned earlier that a male may actually have more feminine energy, while a female can be more masculine. For that reason, the opposite can also be the truth.

Moreover, learn about your partner`s needs. Ask what they admire, and your sexual ritual will be just so much more rich, exciting, healing, and fulfilling. Don`t be afraid to share your needs. There is nothing shameful in having them and expressing yourself honestly.

Also don`t limit the experiences by setting expectations. How can you learn more about your body and feel a higher level of pleasure by constantly setting rules about how everything should go? Expectations can turn into limitations, as they can be transpired from past memories.

Instead, learn to trust your body, heart, and soul to show you the sensations and emotions you have never experienced before. That is exactly when the depth of your connection has the potential to reach its highest level.

Health and Sexuality

One important benefit of sacred sexuality is robust health. When you stop enjoying that essential part of you, you literally send a signal to the brain to start aging. From a nature point of view, one very essential goal of your existence is to reproduce life, which happens through sex.

What I have noticed is that those individuals who honor and practice deep sexual connection are the ones who look and feel much younger and more energized. Those people who lost their interest in this powerful part of them look and feel far less vigorous. Otherwise stated, sexual energy is not only the energy of creation but also of longevity and vitality.

Additionally, a healthy sexual life lowers the risk of prostate cancer, helps regulate menstrual cycles, helps boost fertility, improves the immune system, relieves some types of headaches, and stimulates brain functions. Also, it helps you cope with stress, strengthens the heart, and deepens the connection with your partner.

The Spiral and the Moon

Now that you understand how powerful the area of sexuality is, it is time to practice the new techniques I've introduced. One essential tip I would like to suggest is, during manifestation practices, you should move the energy counterclockwise.

What I mean is, when you would like to create new things, embed new characteristics, or shift your state, feel those new desired qualities and allow them to rise along in a counterclockwise direction around your aura. You can imagine a sparkling light assisting you in this process. As a result, the energy is rising and creating.

You can also use sexual energy to remove blocks, pain, and dark frequencies. In this case, you should feel the energy moving clockwise and washing away all that no longer serves you. For example, you can envision negative qualities or past memories disappearing from your energy field along the clockwise spiral.

This is a very powerful technique that completely transformed my life. It becomes even more effective when you combine it with the cycles of the moon. The best time for manifestation practices is during the growing moon. The best time for elimination of blocks and limitations is during the waning moon. It is my belief that when you follow the cycles of the moon, every earth element begins helping you on your journey.

In conclusion, the next time you decide that there is something shameful about sexual energy, remember that this force is probably the most sacred and divine, as it allows life to continue.

When you accept your sexuality, you awaken the inner power, which in turn makes you more attractive, successful, creative, and present. Your health improves and biological age slows down when you explore and practice this sacred ritual.

Finally, transform into full acceptance, admiration for, and pride in this part of you that is often misunderstood and judged too harshly, and as a result, awaken the undeniable, powerful force of creation within all of your heart's desires.

CHAPTER 5

YOUR BELIEFS CREATE YOUR REALITY

"If you want to change the unwanted patterns in your life, look within to discover their cause."

There are billions of people living in this world, yet it is almost impossible to meet two who are exactly alike. And I am not talking about only their appearances but also their outlook on life. Why are all of us so different? Why do some individuals seem to have everything they desire in life, while others constantly live their life in a state of struggle?

The reason for this phenomenon is that you experience life governed by subconscious beliefs, which are the mental filters that consist of past experiences and memories. Any information that comes into your awareness goes through those filters. Because of this, every individual has a distinct set of beliefs and processes similar information in different ways.

According to Virginia Satir, the famed family therapist, once the information passes through the mental filters, it gets deleted, distorted, or generalized. This process means that you add meaning to the knowledge through the set of unconscious beliefs, which is why evidence of the interpretation is highly subjective.

THE WAY YOU ACQUIRE BELIEFS

How do you create those filters or beliefs? When you are born, you are pure and innocent, and don`t hold any anger or shame, while fully accepting and loving yourself. Then by observing the world around you, you form assumptions based upon that information. Since one`s knowledge as a youngster is limited, you don`t always have a full understanding of how or why anything happens.

Consequently, many of the assumptions—which later become subconscious beliefs—are potentially based on a limited or incorrect understanding of situations. These same beliefs then may turn into limiting factors in your life, and in some cases, you might even argue to defend them. Yet, it is entirely possible that these patterns are no longer serving you.

To say it differently, when you are young, others are in charge of you, and as a result, you are vulnerable and do not always have context to properly understand the occurrences in life. Thus, as a child, you create beliefs not logically, but according to the limited understanding of the emotions as well as from the influence of those around you. That is why it is easy to create unfounded negative beliefs.

As you get older, you subconsciously strengthen those beliefs with patterns of repetitive thoughts and events. Also, you may have mistaken those for your personality and identity. The tricky part is, since the beliefs are unconscious, many people may not be aware of them, so they start blaming life, Higher Power, or even their own environment or circumstances.

Examples of Beliefs

A common illustration of this is when a child born into an abusive family attracts abusive partners later in life, or they themselves act in a violent way toward others, the entire time thinking that this is a normal way to behave or be treated.

Moreover, the person who grew up in poverty may have a tendency to believe that lack is all there is and that they perhaps don't deserve more. This mentality keeps them from knowing how to manifest abundance because of deeply rooted experiences with scarcity. It doesn't matter what work they take on; this poverty-stricken perspective manifests lack due to these incredibly strong limiting beliefs.

I would like to give you an example from my professional experience. My client Jane, 34 years old, had wanted to get married and create a family since she was 23. When we met, she was very close to completely losing hope of ever finding and creating an ideal relationship.

During our hypnotherapy regression sessions in which I guide my clients back into their past for the purpose of uncovering hidden limiting beliefs, we discovered that Jane herself decided at a young age not to get married. She had witnessed her father abusing her mother and assumed that marriage was a painful and heartbreaking experience.

On a conscious level, Jane wanted to build a family more than anything in the world. Despite this, the subconscious beliefs had a deeper hold on her, thereby keeping Jane from manifesting her desire. When she recognized the subconscious issue in the midst of our hypnotherapy session, Jane altered this deeply rooted belief, and from that moment forward, everything shifted in her life.

Another way of understanding subconscious beliefs is to compare them to the script of your life. Some beliefs create abundant and happy scenarios, while others create drama and suffering, which do not allow an individual to rise above limitations and past programming.

COLLECTIVE BELIEFS

Subconscious beliefs are usually acquired from the closest people in one`s childhood, environment, and education. Additionally, some may inherit collective beliefs, which are the common assumptions of people in a specific time and place.

Let`s consider the subject of aging. In the early nineteenth century, in some parts of the world, most people believed that the average life expectancy was forty to forty-two years. Currently, the average life expectancy in the U.S. is around seventy-nine years, which shows us a major increase.

Life expectancy varies in different regions of the world. Some of the variation is due to the environmental conditions of those places and the lifestyle the inhabitants tend to lead. While it is widely accepted that sociological and ecological factors influence life expectancy, let`s examine a few aspects that may reveal the interconnectedness of age and beliefs.

Let`s look at the placebo effect, which has a genuine impact on results no matter the actual medicine used. The way this effect is implemented is by giving a patient some form of medication under the belief that the medicine contains healing properties, when in reality it does not. The patient`s confidence in the remedy is what influences the healing.

As a result, there are numerous people who healed dreadful conditions through the power of faith. Contrarily, there are those who were misdiagnosed, and therefore, believed they were dying, which ultimately led to them passing from seemingly mild conditions. As an American author, Norman Vincent Peale, who popularized the concept of positive thinking, said, "We tend to get what we expect."

What can the placebo effect reveal about collective beliefs? They may possibly shape the way we experience life by assuming the truthfulness of them. Knowing this information, can you be sure that any assumed life span is a fact, rather than a collective belief? A clever quote from a famous baseball player, Satchel Paige, may help you understand this concept: "How old would you be if you didn't know how old you were?"

AGING IS HARD?

Another example of a collective belief is the idea that aging is hard. Some people assume they start aging at thirty. Those individuals usually look and feel old from this point forward. In contrast to this belief, there are those who live a long, healthy life, looking and feeling young well into their eighties.

My dearest friend, Sofia, is currently eighty-seven years old. She feels more youthful and vigorous now than in her teenage years, due to the transformation of her beliefs about aging. In conversations, Sofia often reveals her ideology. She frequently repeats such mantras as, "Every day I am getting healthier, younger, and more beautiful," or "My cells and immune system function optimally," and "I am filled with vital energy."

Another powerful point I would like to introduce to you is the act of examining the question, how *old* are you? Why do you have to be *old*? Instead, ask the question, how *young* are you? This sounds much more powerful in reversing the aging process. Agree?

Losing Someone

The death of a loved one is an experience that might have many ramifications in an individual's life. The burden you may bear, though, is often intensified by societal beliefs. Such an experience can be heartbreaking, yet it will not result in losing the meaning of life if there is no belief in separation.

What I mean is, what if you believe that the essence and soul are eternal? What if the loss of the physical body doesn't truly disconnect you from loved ones on the eternal and spiritual level? Will you feel the same level of sadness, knowing you never truly lose anyone?

That is maybe one of the reasons that some cultures celebrate death. For example, in Mexico there is a tradition called Día de Muertos, which translates as "Day of the Dead." During this holiday, celebrated on the first and second days of November, people remember and celebrate their loved ones who have passed on. This is carried out with joy and belief in an afterlife.

Another collective belief is that separation from a relationship is a painful and heartbreaking experience, that this process will certainly awaken pain and sorrow in one's heart. Yet your belief about how difficult this experience should be will determine its outcome. Any estrangement can be perceived as a loss or a gain.

Unfortunately, divorce in modern society is recognized as something terrifying and, as a result, many people suffer while going through it. What if, instead of believing that a separation is a hurting process, an individual discerns it as the next step in the evolution of their consciousness? In my opinion, any relationship teaches you more about yourself than you would otherwise learn.

Often when you separate from someone, you do it because you realize you no longer share the same interests or values. Your feelings weaken as the distance from each other grows apparent.

When you shift the belief from the idea of losing someone to simply experiencing the next step on your journey, any separation can become a transitional experience. Additionally, when you shift the belief, you do not carry baggage and further limitations into a future relationship.

When attending school, you frequently have the same teachers at each grade. Then when the time comes to go to university, you have progressed to more advanced teachers. Your relationships are your school of life. Some last a lifetime, while others are more temporary. Thus, when you shift how you perceive separation, you transform the experiences.

Negative Habits and Addictions

Some people believe that smoking cigarettes relieves stress, makes them slim, and is a hard habit to quit; these are common beliefs that modern society perpetuates. I know a woman who, despite poor health, continues smoking because she believes that it helps her cope with stress.

How can a substance that can actually cause high blood pressure, heart attack, stroke, and other dreadful conditions release stress? Smoking doesn't eliminate stress. It caused it in the first place. Once a cigarette is finished, the nicotine starts leaving the system and creating a slight withdrawal effect which feels like stress. After inhaling, the smoker satisfies the need, which gives a temporary illusion of relief; after all, smoking is an addiction.

The physical aspect of the dependency is not the main problem, because when an individual stops smoking, the nicotine leaves their system in just three days. What stays is a mental addiction, which is made up of the beliefs of the illusionary benefits of smoking. Once those beliefs are transformed, however, addictions and negative habits are permanently eliminated.

Classification of People

Have you heard expressions that characterize people based on their appearance or nationality? There are billions of people on this earth, and those we are likely to meet will have widely varied qualities and personalities. In my own experience, I have met many people and understand that applying stereotypes in how I think about them would just get in the way of actually knowing who they are as individuals.

And if beliefs project reality, can it be possible that some collective assumptions are strong enough to influence some individuals` destiny? What is also possible is those who associate with cultural collective beliefs and stereotypes are the ones who never even question the truth of those points of view, and therefore, remain ignorant of their own inner power. The good news is that once you realize you create the beliefs, which manifest your experiences, the transformation begins.

Positive Beliefs

Fortunately, not all beliefs place limitations on you. There are empowering ones as well. I knew a boy, Kirill, who grew up in a family who provided him with an excellent education in finance. From an early age, he was introduced to the power of the mind and was taught confidence in accomplishing all of his aspirations. At the age of eighteen, Kirill was already a highly successful businessman who was only at the beginning of his blooming career.

The reason I mention Kirill`s story is to show that an untrained human brain often has a tendency to spend more time on negative information than on positive. Today, after reading this chapter, do not dwell on any limiting beliefs you may have discovered. Rather look for the empowering ones and concentrate on strengthening them. Question all the limiting beliefs as well. And be prepared to transform them in the next chapter.

In conclusion, your beliefs are the mental filters through which you perceive life. If those filters are based on positive and empowering information, you create pleasurable and happy experiences. Nevertheless, if they are clouded with lack and limitation, you may find yourself in a constant loop of struggle.

To say it differently, your beliefs are analogous to a screenplay of the movie that is your life. They build the plot, the foundation, and the direction. The movie characters are the people in your life whose behavior toward you is unconsciously influenced by your beliefs. You are not always consciously aware of that influence, yet your experiences seldom stray far from it.

The magical truth is that you are the author of this script and actually have both the freedom and the power to change it at any time—if you make the conscious choice to do so.

CHAPTER 6

IDENTIFYING AND REMOVING SUBCONSCIOUS BELIEFS

"Transform your beliefs—transform your destiny."

In the previous chapter, you were introduced to subconscious beliefs and how they shape your experiences. In this chapter, I will help you transform limiting beliefs, and as a result, regain the inner power. In order to shift any negative patterns, let's begin with finding them first.

RECOGNIZE SUBCONSCIOUS BELIEFS

1. Observe how you feel in stressful situations. It is one thing to feel prosperous when you have just won the lottery. It is another thing to feel this way when you need to pay bills, especially unexpected ones. It is one thing to feel lovable when you have just received a compliment. It is another thing to feel this way when you are being criticized.

2. Notice similar repeated patterns you have been experiencing, such as unhealthy relationships, accidents, or any negative situations. They are clear indicators of a subconscious belief of not deserving happiness, love, or abundance.
3. Notice the words you use in conversations with yourself and others. For example, an individual with a limiting belief about money may use words such as "It is too expensive," "I can't afford it," or "I can only dream about it." An individual with a limiting belief about self-worth may use words such as "Who am I to have this?" "He will never notice me," or "I am too ordinary to do it." Also, words such as "I hope," "I will try," and "I am not sure," in some situations, are indicators of a limiting belief about competence, as they signify doubts in one's own ability.
4. Notice how much you value the opinions of others. It is healthy to some degree to care what other people think. Nevertheless, individuals with limiting beliefs about self-worth tend to live their lives by a consistent need to be liked and accepted by others and make their choices in accordance with it.
5. Negative excessive and long-lasting emotions such as resentment, pain, anger, fear, and anxiety often occur due to deeply rooted limiting beliefs. Let's say someone with a belief about lack just lost a job. This individual may feel heartbroken and even depressed for weeks or months. Why? Because a person with this type of limiting belief unconsciously always expects lack; that is also possibly why they truly attracted the situation in the first place.

    On the other hand, a person with a strong belief in abundance may perceive the loss of the job as the greatest event that occurred in their life. Realize that if

you believe that everything happens only for the highest good, you will not experience major tragedy or pain in a situation when losing something. You may still experience negative emotions, as they are part of being human, but you will be able to transform them more quickly when powerful beliefs govern your life. And a negative occurrence will not lead to a depression or a prolonged period of sadness, but rather to the next, more powerful chapter of your journey.
6. Jealousy of other people's success is another sign of a limiting belief about competence. If you trust in your own ability to create and manifest your heart's desires, other people's success simply motivates you rather than provokes pessimistic feelings.

Awareness Is Freedom

When you become aware of the self-destructive patterns, the victim mentality dissipates. From now on, you can take full and complete responsibility for your choices and actions. It is essential, though, to put in some work to free yourself from those limitations, so that your life becomes the painting of your creation rather than of the limiting beliefs.

Remember that lessons will keep recurring until subconscious blocks are altered. The more you dismiss the root cause of suffering, the more intense the situations will be to shake you out of ignorance. Why not take control over your destiny and simply remove any causes for hardship? Life is just so much more enjoyable when you live in harmony and abundance.

Steps to Transformation

1. Practice changing your inner monologues.

Who is the person you spend the most time with? It is You. In the mind, you often communicate with yourself. That is why when any limiting belief was first created, it was strengthened and reinforced with your own inner voice. And the words you say to yourself in the present-moment continue to deepen and reaffirm the belief. For that reason, changing the inner monologue from negative to positive will begin creating new pathways in the brain in which a new belief will eventually be formed.

For example, let's say your belief is that money is hard to make. The inner monologue related to that belief can be "I am always losing money," "I will never afford it," "Making money is hard," or another similar one. When negative notions appear, realize they are based on a limiting belief, not on pure facts.

To change this pattern, begin using more empowering statements such as "Money is abundant," "Money flows easily into my life," "I am a magnet for infinite success and affluence." It may not feel truthful for you at first, yet new powerful thoughts combined with the energy exercise I will introduce to you next will soon develop into a new habit which, with enough practice, you won't even have to think about doing. In other words, being abundant will become one of your personality traits.

2. Implement an energetic breathing exercise.

This exercise will interrupt the pattern of limitations if you practice it on a consistent basis. Deep breathing in general takes you back to your natural state, which is peace and wholeness, while energetic breathing will fill you up with a new, more powerful frequency, which will assist you on the path of transformation.

Let's say you work with the limiting belief: I am not enough. Close your eyes for a short moment and envision feeling "enough." How does it feel? You are probably fully satisfied with your appearance, weight, personality, talents, and current circumstances. Feel those emotions intensively and invite them into your energetic field with eight deep breaths. Feel a new level of love and acceptance for yourself in your heart. This way, you are shifting the beliefs on the energetic level.

This exercise may feel forced at first, as this new feeling could be unfamiliar. The more you practice, though, the faster you will take back control of your emotions, break negative patterns, and form new constructive beliefs. This skill will also help you observe your behavior, rather than simply react toward undesirable experiences.

3. Embrace limitations.

Stop resenting limitations. Instead, when they surface, send love toward them. What you resist persists; remember that. Thank those thoughts, feelings, or triggers for coming and reminding you about the existence of the limiting belief. To say it differently, become friends with those occurrences. Afterward, gently remind them to leave.

Would you be friends with someone who brings constant destruction to your world? Probably not. The same is true of limitations. Lovingly send them to reside somewhere else. If they persist, command them to stop or cancel, and stop allowing self-destructive patterns to rule your life.

4. Ask your inner guidance.

Let's say you have a belief that losing weight is hard. As I mentioned earlier, there is always more than one solution to any of life's challenges, and your own intuition often becomes your best teacher and the source of the most effective resolution. Thus, ask a question to your intuition and remain receptive to its guidance. The question could be, "How can I transform a limiting belief about losing weight?"

What is important to know when working with this particular challenge is that extra weight is often the result of a deeply rooted subconscious belief about self-worth. Let me give you an example. A client of mine, Melisa, had struggled to maintain a healthy shape. She asked her guidance and saw a dream a few days later in which her father verbally abused her as a teenager. Melisa also felt compelled to ask me for assistance in order to delve deeper into the cause of the issue.

During our past regression hypnosis, we gathered more details about Melisa's childhood: her father was constantly criticizing her, and her mother did not protect her often enough. Apparently, her father had always wanted to have a boy and had lots of resentment toward his own daughter.

Consequently, as a little girl, Melisa decided that something was wrong with her. As an adult, she attracted this familiar feeling, only in a slightly different form; this time she assumed that something was wrong with her body as a way to distract herself from the bigger issue.

That is why it is so very important to go to the root of the belief in order to transform the external conditions. When Melisa learned to love and accept herself, it became so much easier to manage her weight. The need to overeat and overindulge in unhealthy snacks was miraculously gone, because when you truly love yourself, you learn to treat yourself and your body accordingly.

5. Set a goal to transform your belief.

Let's use a belief, I am not lovable, and learn to transform it by setting a clear goal. Begin by writing down your main objective, which, in this example, is the achievement of full and complete acceptance and self-love. Then discover sub-goals and write them down as well. For example, the sub-goals can be changing the inner monologue, practicing self-love in actions, and shifting limiting energy.

In order to accomplish any objective, develop a consistent approach. The reason why some individuals give up their aspirations is that they decide to climb Mount Everest without proper preparation. Understand that by practicing your new goals for twenty or more minutes a day, consistently over a few weeks' time, you already begin creating new neural pathways in the brain, which eventually will establish a new belief. This new pattern will get stronger and more powerful the more you practice new skills, and eventually it will destroy the limiting concept, since your subconscious mind can't hold opposing beliefs.

To create the plan of improvement, you can write on a piece of paper three or more new things you will do daily to reach the objective. When I was transforming the belief that "I am unlovable" my list looked like this:

> Today I will work to alter any limiting self-talk, and I will remind myself as often as possible how magnificent, beautiful, and talented I am.
>
> I will take deep breaths of pure love for myself, fill every cell of my body, and recharge my emotions with them.
>
> I will take some time to indulge myself in the bath or enjoy a healthy dinner with my best friend.

6. Become aware of your spoken word.

What do you frequently say about yourself or about life in conversations with others? Expressions such as "Bad things always happen to me," "I constantly lose things," "I am not good at this," or other similar ones are clear indicators of a limiting belief.

In this example, let's again compare your life with a movie script, which is written under the influence of the spoken words, which are the result of your beliefs. To shift those convictions, rewrite the script by implementing new empowering stories about yourself.

While in conversation with others, for example, stop using pessimistic sentences. Instead start talking about abundance and infinite possibilities. Start living your ideal life in the now. No, you are not lying—you are recreating yourself. And besides, by sharing positive messages, you simultaneously uplift others.

7. Learn to accept compliments with ease and grace

Your inability to receive a compliment strengthens a limiting belief about self-worth, as your subconscious mind takes everything precisely. Let's say someone says, "Wow, you've come a long way since we first met!" If you reply, "Don't say that" in an attempt to be humble, you are sending a message to the subconscious: "I have not advanced," which your mind accepts as a fact, and with enough repetition, will manifest events that take you a step backward in your progress. Do you really need to slow down your expansion?

8. Eliminate limiting beliefs by noticing your triggers.

Observe yourself or ask your closest friends to help you find out what negatively affects your emotions. As a simple example, let's say you get triggered while being criticized. In this situation, many unpleasant emotions probably rise to the surface.

Realize that the negative reaction is coming from a limiting belief such as "Something is wrong with me," "Nobody loves me," or "I don`t deserve love." When you have a strong powerful belief about self-worth, criticism doesn`t completely unravel you, because you know who you are, and the need for others to decide it for you disappears.

You can alter the belief by changing the reaction, which will eventually interrupt the habitual pattern and lead to a positive response. To do so, the next time you feel triggered, I recommend taking eight deep breaths of love, smiling, reading a passage in a book, or anything you would usually not do in this situation. And give rise to the new positive belief in your life.

There`s one important thing I would like to add. If someone criticizes you, there is possibly still a pattern in your attracting condemnation. The other person or situation is simply a mirror of your inner world. *In other words, others often speak to you the way you speak with yourself.* So instead of getting frustrated, bless the experience, and say thank you to the one who brought it to your attention.

9. Reconnect with your inner child.

This technique means reconnecting with yourself when you were a little child. It is very powerful because the limiting belief was acquired in the early stages of development, and despite the fact you are already an adult, that wounded inner child is still often talking and reacting through you in times when you are triggered and in distress.

Now close your eyes if it is needed, look at your inner child`s eyes, and tell them, "I love you, you are beautiful, you are lovable." "You deserve to manifest all of your heart`s desires." "You are capable of accomplishing what you set your mind to do." Use any encouragements that are relevant to your situation.

In addition, feel the inner child with you constantly, take them for a walk, nurture them, compliment them, give them a hug, and encourage them; do anything they need to feel loved and accepted. The more often you practice this exercise, the faster you will alter limiting beliefs.

10. Use affirmations.

How many different activities do you usually perform during the day such as driving, washing dishes, taking a shower, or exercising? Why not use this time productively and speak affirmations during those moments? The indicated statements are most effective when they provoke feelings, so practice them with your heart rather than only with your mind.

To discover the most powerful affirmations, write down negative words you use to describe yourself and your experiences, and then write down the opposite ones. Let's say you often voice "I have an addictive personality." Now instead say, "I can easily transform all addictions." Please do not call addictions and limiting beliefs your own. They are no longer yours; remember, you are *done* with them.

11. Eliminate negative words.

While altering limiting beliefs, do not use words such as *losing*, *not*, and *stopping*. When you say *losing* weight, or *losing* any habit, it may feel as if you are depriving yourself of something instead of gaining and benefiting from its absence.

If you instead imprint a belief, such as, *My body is slim, athletic, healthy, and vibrant,* you not only stop gaining weight or abusing your body with poisonous substances; you also positively influence

Identifying and Removing Subconscious Beliefs

its wellness and vitality. When you use the word *not*, you weaken the meaning of what you are saying. For example, *I am not sick* loses its power in comparison to *I am vibrant*.

12. Visualize new beliefs.

Visualize yourself as already being governed by a powerful paradigm. Let`s use as an example a belief "Love is hard to find." An individual with a similar view should visualize how easily love flows into their life. Specifically, they should visualize being noticed, admired, and loved, and feel control over this matter. This way, a new positive belief will be imprinted in the subconscious mind. Once this happens, *you* will manifest your aspirations.

13. Use self-hypnosis.

Your beliefs were created unconsciously, and therefore, the fastest way to transform them is by targeting them through the subconscious mind. Self-hypnosis is a form of meditation in which you relax your body and mind, using suggestions and imagery to release the past, improve concentration, boost confidence, change negative beliefs and, as a result, simply become more successful and fulfilled.

Self-hypnosis is best achieved when you learn how to tune in to alpha or theta brain waves, the states when you feel completely relaxed, similar to falling asleep, while simultaneously being fully aware. That is when you can discover and alter limiting subconscious beliefs, as you tap into a different memory compartment of the brain.

You can achieve that state any time during the day. Do not be afraid to be sleepy and tired after this practice, as the more relaxation is attained, the more energized and rested you become.

The state is so powerful that often those who didn't receive enough sleep immediately feel revitalized.

In order to achieve it, find a peaceful, comfortable place such as a chair, bed, or sofa. You can turn on tranquil music that can help you drift into a pleasant, dreamy state. To do self-hypnosis, simply remember the text in your own words and guide yourself through this practice.

Hypnosis

Start taking deep breaths, close your eyes and say to yourself, "I am feeling more and more relaxed with every breath I take." Give suggestions to every part of your body. For example, you can command your head, face, neck, chest, arms, and other parts to relax. While keeping your eyes closed, look up and then quickly return them to a normal position. Looking up is very important since it helps you reach the subconscious mind. Now ask your powerful mind to help you discover and transform limiting beliefs and be open to receive powerful insights.

Afterward imagine yourself walking down a staircase toward a mysterious room or a place within you, where limiting patterns reside. During self-hypnosis, this space can be envisioned in various ways: an area full of light, an alchemist's laboratory, or a simple everyday room. In the course of self-hypnosis, continue taking deep breaths, as this practice will assist you in becoming more relaxed.

While walking on the staircase, you can take three steps, or you can take a hundred steps. It depends on the depth of your relaxation. Another way to get to that mysterious space is by counting backward. For example, you may count down from thirty to one, and with each step, command your body and mind to become more tranquil.

When you feel fully relaxed, think back to a scene from your childhood. Notice where you are and observe as many details as possible such as the walls around you and whether you are by yourself or with others. If you are not alone, who are those people around you? What are they doing? How do they make you feel? What did they teach you about life? If you are alone, discern how you feel. What causes you to experience those emotions?

If nothing comes to mind, remember the room in your childhood and any scene that triggered negative emotions. How young are you? How do you feel? If still nothing comes to mind, don't push it. Instead ask your intuitive guidance to assist you in this process. The reason you might find it difficult to enter this state is because you're afraid to reach a deeper revelation of your past at this moment, or you might not be able to enter a peaceful alpha or theta state on your own just yet.

For those who are able to access the depth of their subconscious, realize that as adults we often forget some dramatic and intense experiences that happened in childhood and which may have resulted in the formation of a self-destructive belief.

Therefore, when the scene becomes more vivid, be your own detective and ask yourself this question: "What did I assume about myself due to that experience?" Know that you possibly formed a belief as a result of this event, but you did it with only the limited knowledge and understanding you had at the time. Transform that belief by implementing and affirming a new powerful vision of yourself. If you feel like experiencing any emotions such as anger, sadness, or pain, don't hold them in. By feeling those emotions fully, you are releasing them.

The next step is to forgive the people from your childhood who may have influenced limiting concepts. Forgiveness is the greatest medicine for the soul, so please spend as much time as needed on this powerful practice. Realize that those who taught you the negative belief or hurt you in any way were simply the teachers on your journey and possibly helped you evolve and build positive qualities. Most of the time, due to those experiences, you became wiser, stronger, and more powerful. Also understand that only hurt people hurt others. So, if someone caused suffering in you, just think about the amount of pain they were experiencing. To forgive others, envision them in front of you and give them a hug. Say to them, "I forgive you; I release you, and I set you free." Stay with them until you feel a release in the heart.

Now feel and see your inner child. Envision them sitting in front of you. Hug the inner child and promise from now on you will only love and support them. This beautiful child is always in your heart and needs your love and attention more than anyone else in the world. Forgive yourself for past mistakes by saying, "I love you; I forgive you, and I release that experience." Stay in this moment until you feel serenity and unconditional love in the heart. Accept that you are enough, and you will always be enough. You are wonderful. You are worthy of love. You are abundant. And you are an infinite creator. Amplify those emotions and promise the inner child to stop any self-criticism, and from now on, only to provide encouragement and emotional support.

Stay with the inner child as much as needed, until only love and abundance radiate from your heart. Afterward, begin counting from one to five. On the count of five, you are wide awake, transformed, and ready to experience life as a new, *more powerful you*.

Your Path to Mastery

Some people work on themselves for a few minutes a day and expect to see results. Again, ask yourself the following question: How much would I like to live an extraordinary life? Each of us has about eight to fourteen active hours each day. How are you spending this precious time?

Understand that your inner state in the present moment reflects your future reality, and if in the present you are reliving the hurdles of the past, then you are recreating them in the future. You become what you are most often doing and feeling on a consistent basis. Remember, there are only two ways of living your life; one is as an infinite and abundant creator, and the other is as a loyal servant to subconscious limitations. *Choose the path wisely.*

In conclusion, to shift limiting beliefs, you should become aware of your inner monologues, triggers, spoken words, and repeated patterns, and put in the work to transform them. By creating new constructive habits such as encouraging yourself, deepening connection with the inner child, altering your energy, and practicing affirmations, you are instilling a new paradigm in the mind. Since your beliefs reside in the subconscious, one effective way to shift them is through a hypnotic state of consciousness.

Repetition is the key when it comes to transforming any patterns, so please constantly remind yourself that *you are not the limiting beliefs, rather, you are the creator of your destiny*. Continue practicing these profound techniques to build a *new you* that is an example of effortless manifestation and high-vibrational energy. Feel unconditional gratitude for all the progress you have already made, and do not forget to notice what a miracle YOU truly are!

PART III
ACHIEVE PERSONAL GREATNESS

CHAPTER 7
MASTER YOUR SELF-IMAGE

"What you think you are, you truly are."

Positive self-image is an essential step for your growth, success, and fulfillment, since reality is directly connected with how you view and perceive yourself. I previously mentioned in the chapter "Your Beliefs Create Your Reality" how you first create beliefs and then those patterns reflect your experiences. Self-image is a form of belief about yourself that can either serve or harm you.

When you have a positive and powerful self-image, you navigate life effortlessly. In contrast, when someone has a fatalistic view of themselves, they invite self-imposed suffering. To put it differently, self-image is confidence in one's own ability or character, which must be strong in order to live a fulfilled and successful life.

We all have an inner voice inside us. There is a big difference, though, between a person with a positive self-image and a person with a low opinion of themself. The first one masters their inner voice to speak only encouragingly and constructively about themself and their abilities. The second one tends to diminish and criticize themself, which often leads to missed opportunities and rejections.

Negative Inner Talk

The way you talk to yourself affects not only the way you feel but also your health, level of success, productivity, and motivation. Additionally, negative inner talk makes you weaker. To see this in action, you can experiment with a friend or a family member.

Stretch your hand forward and extend it with pressure while saying positive and uplifting words to yourself and ask someone to push the hand down. While you are saying positive words, your hand should remain tight. Now try the same exercise, but this time, say negative statements about yourself. You will be amazed how easy it is for your hand to be pushed down.

The same principle is applied in life. When your self-image is negative, it is easy to slip into drama and hardship, because even a small negative remark may lead to anxiety and enormous pain. Conversely, a positive and encouraging self-image leads to an unshakable strength that comes from accepting and believing in oneself.

Accept Yourself

Some individuals strive to become someone else while creating a positive self-image, because they admire an *ideal* person they want to be like. Realize that millions of years of evolution did not occur to create you perfectly only so that you could doubt the process. Therefore, a powerful self-image is not about becoming the next Bruce Lee, Nikola Tesla, or Audrey Hepburn. It is about falling in love with your own qualities and talents and eliminating fears of fully expressing them.

The qualities and talents I am talking about do not have to be defined by the norms of society. For example, Arnold Schwarzenegger has a very thick Austrian accent that was not beneficial to his acting career according to many Hollywood experts. Yet he decided to see it as a uniqueness and strength rather than a weakness, and as a result, it didn't stop Schwarzenegger from achieving success; on the contrary, his accent is exactly what made him distinctive and recognizable.

Fear of Rejection

How often do you stop doing something because you are afraid of the pain of rejection? It is because low self-image and fear of rejection go hand in hand. I would like to give you an example. At the time we met, a client of mine, Tracy, was married to an abusive and cruel man.

She shared with me that there was a kind and successful man at work who showed her signs of affection. On a conscious level, Tracy knew that Martin, the coworker, was a much better partner for her, yet she continued staying with her abusive husband. During our hypnotherapy sessions, Tracy became clear that, more than anything in the world, she was afraid of being abandoned since that was all she had experienced as a child.

Tracy was so afraid of that pain, she would not even allow an idea of closeness with Martin, as deep inside she felt inferior to him and expected to be abandoned. By not receiving enough love and attention in childhood, her low self-image was born. Tracy decided she was not worthy of love, success, and happiness, and her abusive husband was a clear demonstration of that limiting image of self.

Can you see now how low self-image and various fears are interconnected? It is the fear of being rejected, abandoned, accused, or disliked that keeps people behaving small and missing out on precious opportunities. On the contrary, when you are in harmony with yourself, you are not deeply affected by rejections and criticism, and as a result, stop fearing and attracting them.

Something that can help you greatly is the realization that rejection often has nothing to do with you. Let's say you are choosing a dress for a birthday party. You are given various options, yet you only buy one or two. Is something wrong with the other dresses? No, you simply like and prefer your favorite ones based on your own judgment.

When someone rejects you, it is their choice, a choice that has a lot to do with their life's circumstances, personal taste, or any other cause, rather than you. So truly see rejection as God's protection and release all unnecessary suffering that comes with it.

Prevent Pain

Realize that one of the mind's functions is to prevent you from experiencing pain, and that is why it is often easy to stay within your comfort zone. If you have a low self-image, the immense fear of emotional pain may lead you to miss out on golden opportunities. When you have a positive self-image, this pattern weakens.

When something does not go according to plan, an individual with a positive self-image doesn't get stuck in blame, guilt, or other negative feelings. This person is more prone to being optimistic as they transform the illusion of pain. For that reason, challenges no longer hold their entire attention and get transformed into a beautiful lesson.

The marvelous thing is that certain closed doors of opportunity may have actually protected you from unfavorable outcomes.

And when you realize that everything in life happens for a divine reason, you regain power over life's challenges and transmute negativity.

SELF-IMAGE AND YOUR APPEARANCE

In the book *Psycho-Cybernetics*, which was written by Maxwell Maltz, a plastic surgeon, there is a chapter on self-image, which mentions that most plastic surgeries will not be necessary if a person shifts their image of themselves.

Some individuals decide to find perfection and strengthen their self-image through changing their appearance. Yet, unless self-love and self-acceptance emerge from within, external change will not create positive results. It is like masking the symptoms, rather than working directly with the cause.

Neale Donald Walsch, American author of *Conversations with God*, has an interesting quote that reveals a powerful way of perceiving reality: "Quantum physics tells us that nothing that is observed is unaffected by the observer. That statement holds an enormous and powerful insight. It means that everyone sees a different truth because everyone is creating what they see."

What a profound concept. It is not what you look at; it is what you see while glancing at it. Realize, observing is also an act of creation. Starting today, look at yourself with unconditional love and acceptance, and as a result, create a new YOU. Also, what you see in yourself, you radiate into the world. That is why, if you have created an ideal shape of your nose, face, and body with the help of plastic surgery and are unable to see the beauty within, those acts didn't add allure to your image; rather, they added more cause for self-criticism and doubt.

As you can see, questioning and examining assumptions is a recurring theme throughout this book. It is essential because in order to stop being a victim of limiting beliefs, you must become aware of them first. Moreover, by transforming those limitations, you open the door for inner power and infinite potential to emerge.

STEPS TO A WINNING SELF-IMAGE

1. Create a new, constructive image of you.

You always have a choice about whether to concentrate on positive or negative qualities. It starts with believing that life should not be excruciating and there is absolutely nothing wrong with you.

What you focus on is what you make manifest. For that reason, shift your attention toward positivity, and a new positive reality will be designed. Continue expanding this new perspective of your being and embark on producing magnificent results.

2. Use your vision book as a source of the desired image of yourself.

Find images that portray a confident, successful, and radiant you. Attach them to a page in your new vision book and look at them daily. Feel what it is like to be that person. What is it like to relish life from this great outlook?

The more you feel and experience this new way of being, the more motivation and insights you will receive to master a powerful self-image. It is also an effective learning opportunity to consistently evolve to the next level, as you can change those images whenever you progress to the next step.

3. Say positive affirmations looking at yourself in the mirror.

Louise Hay, a famous self-love coach, used a mirror technique to transform a negative self-image. When you look into your eyes in the mirror, it is believed you can communicate with the subconscious mind. What are you seeing? Beauty and magnificence or flaws and imperfections?

Please remind yourself to see and notice the beauty within and to encourage and compliment yourself. This effective practice will assist you in creating a powerful self-image and awaken bliss and inner satisfaction.

4. Find time for self-care.

It is one thing to transform the inner talk, but it is another to show yourself love through daily actions. Rest when you feel tired. Treat yourself to a spa or do whatever your soul is wishing for to demonstrate how much you care about and love YOU. Realize that giving yourself time to rest transforms you into a happier, younger, healthier, and more productive person.

5. Accept your appearance.

Remember, beauty is an abstract idea. What one person thinks is attractive may not be so for another. If you believe there is something wrong with you, even if you are the most beautiful person on earth, you will send signals to other people and project those imperfections.

Ultimately, if you have a low self-image, you will never be fully satisfied with your appearance no matter what you do. Consequently, shift from self-judgments to self-love to create more blissful experiences. Remember that beauty is not how you look but rather what you radiate about yourself and your qualities.

You probably know of celebrities who have chosen eccentric looks. They did this because simplicity is not always interesting. The reason you may judge and see some of your qualities as negative is that you have not yet realized that those so-called imperfections can actually make you distinctive and special. Just as no two snowflakes are identical, humans are all different, and their beauty lies in their dissimilarities.

6. Observe your conversations with others.

Do you use words that diminish you in any way? Remember you are what you believe you are, and spoken words are the best way to reveal your view of yourself. Is it easy for you to speak constructively about yourself? Is it enjoyable for you to speak of your greatest achievements?

Realize that there is nothing wrong with sharing positivity when the intention is right. And when you love and appreciate yourself, it becomes easy to express yourself authentically and stop second-guessing your choices.

If speaking upliftingly about yourself is still challenging, practice until it becomes a new normal. What I also notice is that the most self-critical people are the ones who find faults in others the most. So, by learning to speak positively about yourself, you also start seeing more beautiful qualities in others. This way, so many conflicts and negativity can be abolished from your life and the world.

In conclusion, a positive self-image is the key to success in every endeavor. Self-image is shaped by your childhood experiences and is the direct path toward a life of transformation or of self-destruction.

Fortunately, you are in control of altering the direction by setting free the inner critic, creating a new loving relationship with yourself, transforming your self-expression, and discovering time for self-care. Also, by using a vision book and incorporating affirmations you can surely accelerate your progress as well.

Life is an invigorating adventure when you are governed by a constructive self-image. Please continue embracing your true marvelous self by reawakening your inner power and begin experiencing a reality of boundless possibilities.

CHAPTER 8

DEVELOP YOUR WILLPOWER

*"Your destiny is shaped by your
daily choices and decisions."*

What comes to mind when you think about the word "willpower"? Many would define it as the ability to force yourself to do something that you don't necessarily want to do but need to accomplish. This is often even viewed as a noble skill to which everyone should aspire.

In truth, forcing is actually going *against* the will, rather than empowering it. Through that repetition, you can actually weaken your drive. Pushing yourself to do something implies force. And in this context, a consistent practice of pushing yourself to do something does not always produce satisfying results.

That is because when you do fail to accomplish the desired outcome, for instance, you may now develop a belief that you have no willpower. By contrast, strengthening your will comes not from forcing yourself to do something, but rather from tapping into an inspiration to pursue the desired outcomes.

Not forcing yourself is not the same as being lazy or avoiding responsibilities. Pursuing your goals is vital for achieving success, but what is important is to make sure that the objectives you choose to pursue are in alignment with your subconscious beliefs. Otherwise, you are simply exerting effort, which can be wasted if you are investing the energy in the wrong direction.

Power of Will

What you need to know when working on strengthening your willpower is that everything in life should be in balance. Another way of looking at it: too much restriction is as negative as too much indulgence. For example, your so-called bad habits may not necessarily be harmful if done in moderation. It is overdoing anything that can bring detrimental results. This is why it is important to be able to say yes or no to certain things. Just to clarify, that doesn't mean that addictions to drugs or destructive habits are okay to do in moderation.

Realize that life turns into an extraordinary journey when you learn to make the right choices for your well-being. The essential difference is when you force yourself to change as opposed to when you discover the power within to change. The word willpower actually has the word "power" in it. Simply put, learn to strengthen the inner power rather than forcing yourself.

According to many willpower experiments, those who practiced force intensely during a short period of time actually depleted their will and became even more easily swayed. When you use the inner power, contrariwise, your willpower never becomes depleted. Quite the opposite; it only multiplies with the proper use.

Having the inner power aligned also offers the benefit of being able to disregard what is not beneficial for you with ease. After all, power is a realization and application of your ability to transform and shift any negative and limiting patterns without forcing the process and feeling depleted.

Approach Through Power

Let me give you an example of someone who is stuck in a constant attempt to lose weight. This individual has tried to do so through forcing themselves, which resulted in quitting the desired task multiple times. How could you approach this goal by utilizing inner power?

First, realize that your weight may have less to do with food and exercise (which are also influencing factors) and more to do with your self-esteem level. What I mean is, people who have confidence in their own worth do not find themselves out of shape. This is because they are connected with their bodies, and that positive personal view of themselves is the reason why they have a high motivation to exercise and eat right.

Interestingly enough, when you meet this type of person, you may be sure they have strong willpower to make the right health choices. And it is very true. It is just that their willpower comes from their powerful self-image, so making the right choices becomes second nature.

Conversely, when the image of yourself is poor, it starts to be reflected in mistreatment of yourself and your body. People affected by this pattern may claim that they have low willpower while, in truth, they simply haven't yet found the power within to accept and love themselves.

Willpower and Limiting Beliefs

Procrastination, for example, is often believed to be a lack of willpower. Nevertheless, in most cases, it is simply the outcome of a limiting belief in one`s own ability to accomplish something. When you are inspired, when you live your dreams vigorously, procrastination only occurs from time to time. And in this case, it can actually be a sign to rest and recharge, as a lot of inspired leaders forget to rest sometimes.

Let me give an example of one of my clients, Samuel, who was challenged by procrastination. For many years, he felt stuck as his actions just didn`t seem to follow his desires. Samuel wanted to continue his family restaurant business, yet he could not awaken enough motivation to commit to the meetings and follow through with the required work. At the time I met Samuel, he had lost any faith in willpower and the ability to accomplish the desired goal.

I knew deep inside that the issue had little to do with willpower, as it was simply the outcome of the negative pattern within. I advised Samuel to do Rapid Transformational Hypnotherapy to discover the root cause of the issue. During the hypnosis, we discovered that in childhood his older brother got most of the attention and appreciation from their parents.

Samuel`s parents showed more belief in the older brother due to his outgoing and bright personality. As a young adult, Samuel did not feel worthy of success, which he simply projected in a pattern of procrastination. Once we began working on this subconscious block, Samuel started waking up before the alarm sounded and easily found the inspiration to do the work. He continued strengthening a new belief, which was "I am successful, lovable, and talented." The more Samuel practiced replacing the old program, the faster his inner power grew while the need to force himself was disappearing.

Can you see how deeply limiting beliefs can weaken willpower? In the previous chapters, "Your Beliefs Create Your Reality" and "Identifying and Removing Subconscious Beliefs," we explored the journey of freedom from all limitations. Please continue transforming negative beliefs and removing the misconception that your willpower is weak. Instead discover the root cause of undesirable patterns.

Willpower and Repetition

When you repeat something over and over again, it eventually becomes a part of your personality. Let's say it's hard for you to say no to people, even when it creates challenges in your life. You know this behavior hurts your productivity and adds undue anxiety, yet you remain stuck in this habit. You may even believe that you have no willpower to say no to others.

To change this pattern, start incorporating small manageable steps. You don't have to reach the top of the highest mountain in the pursuit of saying no. Here is one technique you can implement. If you find yourself stretched too thin because you overcommit to others, start replying, "I will help you with this particular task, but I can only stay for a short period of time today."

On the next occasion, shorten the time even more, and continue doing so until this new way of responding becomes your new normal. If it feels scary to give such a reply, practice it in the mirror or with a pet first. After all, what do you have to lose? Nothing. Perform this new skill repeatedly until you have gained confidence and respect not only for yourself but from others as well.

Willpower and Negative Habits

Have you ever asked yourself, "How do I develop negative habits, and why do I encounter challenges in the process of changing them?" Let's say you are often late, and at this point, this action has turned into consistent behavior.

Then, when you attempt to break free from this habit using willpower, you may notice how ineffective it is. Again, mastering willpower through inner power is much more effective than forcing yourself to do something. So, look within to find the deep underlying pattern that is perpetuating this type of behavior.

It could be that deep inside you carry a self-limiting belief in your own abilities, which is why you sabotage yourself by arriving late. Another reason could be that one of your parents had similar traits that you took on from childhood. Or possibly you may have a deep-seated disdain for life, which manifests itself as an outward resentment and causes you to frequently arrive late. So before questioning your willpower, discover and transform the root cause of unwanted habits, and the inspiration for a better behavior will be naturally awakened.

Also, if you hold a similar pattern, begin practicing new powerful affirmations such as these: "I am always on time. I am inspired to do great things. I respect other people's time." Set reminders to implement these statements daily until they live and breathe in your personality. Shift your attention from the limiting quality to the results you will gain and start feeling those new outcomes as already being manifested to create profound changes.

Willpower and Addictions

Some people believe that they have low willpower because they have a hard time saying no to addictive substances. Realize that when your body is craving a certain toxin, you may feel that you have no strength to control the desire.

What actually happens, though, is the substance creates new pathways in the brain that lead to a sense of hunger. And when you feel hungry, a natural instinct would be to consume more of what you wish to have. This process influences a strong substance dependence both for body and mind.

To deal with any addiction, you should understand the effects those substances have on the brain and begin questioning the truthfulness of the craving. Afterward, discover the true cause of that need. Drug addiction is often the outcome of limiting subconscious beliefs and the result of a restless and untamed mind. By not treating that cause, it is very challenging to eliminate the dependence due to the consistent, unconscious, and unsatisfied need for the substance, which may create an assumption that you have no willpower.

On the contrary, when the true reason for the addiction is healed and the illusions of pleasure from it are abolished, no force will be required to reject the detrimental choices.

Harmful Ingredients

Did you know that the level of glucose in your blood can affect your willpower? Any food provides glucose to your brain. Yet, unhealthy choices such as refined sugar, corn syrup, and artificial sweeteners will cause a spike of glucose but only for a short period of time, after which, your glucose level actually crashes. At that moment, you may experience a lack of energy and, as a result, low willpower.

How do you crush the addiction to those foods? One good piece of advice is to perform the task of eating unhealthy choices differently. If you are addicted to candy and frequently overeat it, one way to slow yourself down is to use your non-dominant hand while snacking. And instead of calling it candy, call it something with a personal negative connotation, such as "diabetes bites," "cavity producers," or "cellulite enhancers."

What is important to remember while working on strengthening your willpower is to make a conscious choice instead of the automatic unconscious one. Willpower is a daily practice, after all, and like a fit body, grows stronger over time.

Every time you catch yourself using negative words that imply you are incapable of accomplishment, stop and remember that those are not facts, rather *the beliefs* that were previously imprinted into your subconscious mind. People often confuse their beliefs with their personality traits without realizing that they are simply memorized and frequently repeated behaviors. With this awareness, you are a step closer to the personal liberation of self.

Reminders and Willpower

While you are working on willpower, reminders are important. You have probably experienced in the past the abandonment of newfound goals and dreams. It happened because the old patterns won. For example, let`s say you spend lots of useless time on the phone, and your goal is to eliminate this behavior. When you previously set this intention, it worked, but only for a few days until the old habit took over.

What if you had set reminders of the benefits you would gain from the elimination of this unwanted way of acting? Do you think the outcome could have been different? It would be. Remember, the reason the pattern strengthened was due to its extended repetition. That is why placing the reminders of the benefits in noticeable places will evoke new behaviors by gradually instilling the new positive belief in the subconscious mind, which will get stronger over time.

A powerful question may also be a great incentive: "How much would you like to transform your life?" Some individuals take a long time committing to making changes to destructive patterns. They often feel in the moment that life will last forever and that they will have many more years to incorporate positive habits. Realize that procrastinating in making changes strengthens limiting beliefs and keeps you from reaching your highest potential. *Moreover, make a decision today to alter your life!*

PEACEFUL MIND

Throughout this book, I mention that your mind, unless it is properly used, may cause various complications. That is why learning meditation and stillness are essential practices. You will soon learn how important it is to find the middle ground between stillness of the mind and positive thinking.

What is essential to understated at this moment is that overthinking depletes your energy, and when that happens, you are more likely to create undesirable consequences. Let`s say you have been contemplating repeatedly during the day about your past, future, recurring problems, or all the things that are causing a constantly stimulated mind. As time in the day escapes, you feel tired, and decide to skip important tasks that were previously prioritized.

Now you may believe that you have low willpower, while truly you simply exhausted your vital energy. That happened because a busy mind is one of the reasons many people are suffering from fatigue and procrastination, as it consumes a large amount of mental fuel.

The outcome in this particular situation could have been different if you had taken some time to meditate and be fully present. To say it differently, if you achieved a state of detachment from your own thoughts, even for twenty minutes, it would have resulted in a more restful mind, body, and spirit, as well as increased energy and motivation.

In conclusion, I would like to remind you that the most effective way to strengthen your willpower is not through force but rather through personal power and potential. Weak willpower is often the consequence of a limiting belief, lack of passion, or depleted energy rather than a part of your identity.

Compelling willpower will naturally be reborn once you discover the root cause for the lack of motivation or of certain unwanted behaviors. And a peaceful mind is the key to stop depleting your vital energy and instead utilize it to pursue your goals with naturally risen power and determination.

CHAPTER 9

ELIMINATE FEARS FROM YOUR LIFE

"There is no illusion greater than fear."
— Lao Tzu

Fear is such a dominating emotion within modern society that I would like to devote a whole chapter to it. Recently I traveled to Costa Rica, where I learned how accurate the expression *you create your reality* truly is. I am sure you are familiar with the idea that your mindset is very powerful. Yet, an average person thinks about seventy thousand thoughts a day. Do you actually manifest all those notions? It is evident that you do not.

You do, however, manifest those thoughts that have the biggest impact on your feelings; and fears are the negative thoughts that frequently overpower the peace and harmony of one's heart. That being said, I would like to share a story of how I manifested my fears.

Costa Rican Beetles

All my life, I have been afraid of beetles, especially large black ones. This spring I traveled to Costa Rica, and at one point during the trip I stayed at my friend's house in the jungle, in a very famous town, Jaco.

Costa Rica has probably one of my favorite climates on earth. The air is so very warm, fresh, moist, and filled with ozone since it rains daily in the summer. Unfortunately, I was not the only one who loved that perfect tropical rain climate. All kinds of insects love that environment as well, and among them, big black beetles.

When I first arrived at my friend's house, I could not believe how many different insects I encountered. In the first five minutes of being outside near his home, I was stung by a black wasp, which created a stinging sensation that lasted for about fifteen minutes.

By the evening that day, my arms and legs had an enormous number of red dots. It felt like some invisible crawlers were on my body all the time. I asked my friend how to prevent those bites. After saying, "Welcome to the jungle," he gave me some natural herbal oils that actually helped. I was so grateful and relieved and was ready to experience the true magic of Costa Rica.

When I woke up the next morning, I was in an incredible mood, singing with the birds. I was so happy, I felt like I wanted to embrace the entire world. In the evening, though, a black beetle landed on my shoulder. I screamed and even started shaking from disgust. That beetle was probably my biggest fear on earth.

In that moment of anguish, I actually decided to leave the jungle house. Immediately afterward, a second thought arrived: What about all my planned adventures in Jaco? I said to myself, "That creature, which was not even the size of my palm, won't ruin my plans." So, I decided to stay.

The fear of the beetles, nevertheless, did not disappear. Just the sound of something buzzing made me frantic. The next day went by quickly, yet was like a rollercoaster. The fear got stronger and stronger as I encountered many more beetles, and one of them was about to land on my head. I even started waking up during the night to ensure there were not any beetles in my bed. Tragically, the fear began preventing me from sleeping peacefully. But that was only the beginning.

At this point, I was seriously thinking of moving to my next destination, La Fortuna, a beautiful hot springs spot. Nevertheless, I felt kind of embarrassed about what was sending me away. I reminded myself how many more exhilarating events were planned in Jaco and how foolish it would be to leave because of those black beetles. Thus, I decided to stay.

Despite the fact, though, that the adventures in Jaco were magical, the fear continued to grow, and it seemed like the number of beetles in my vicinity was increasing as well. It was my third day there, and we had some guests coming over for dinner that night. When our friends arrived, we shared a wonderful dinner. We laughed, we talked, and had the time of our lives.

Honestly, I think people in Costa Rica have very special and open-hearted souls which are impossible not to love. Anyhow, at one moment during the dinner I happened to look at my plate and noticed a big black beetle roasted in the veggies. "Oh my God," I thought, struggling to hide my shock from the guests. I passed the food under the table to the cat, as I did not want to interfere with my friends` appetites. It was honestly a shocking and life-changing moment. "How could that beetle appear in the food?" I thought. Then I suddenly realized how I had manifested my most intense fear by giving it my whole attention.

At one moment during a conversation, I asked my friends what they thought about insects in Costa Rica. As I mentioned earlier, my friends were local, and they told me that those insects rarely bother them, nor do those beetles come to them. As a matter of fact, the owner of the house informed me he had never seen such a copious number of beetles coming to his home.

It confirmed even deeper in my soul that my fear of them did attract those beetles to me. In other words, I had invited them into my world. I later related this story to other fears and negative thoughts, and it was a wake-up call for me to shift limiting thoughts immediately and instead choose only those notions that served my emotional well-being.

The Birth of Fear

Realize that the inner voice that speaks fears to you actually exists to serve and protect you. For instance, while cooking a delicious dinner, this voice would remind you not to grab the pan out of the oven with bare hands. That guidance exists to protect you from harmful situations. Unfortunately, the same inner voice can fabricate terrors in otherwise safe surroundings.

It is easy to understand why modern society seems to be addicted to fears and suffering. It is enough to turn on the television or look at a local newspaper where you will find lots of negative and frightening messages. Those messages in the modern world appear much more frequently than the positive ones.

Movies that portray human suffering and violence seem to be the norm of this time. Evidently, fearful information seems to be a necessary ingredient to keep audiences engaged and sell both movies and news stories. Tragically, all of these facts create a negative imprint on the subconscious mind.

In addition to negative media, some learn fears from their parents or the environment they grew up in. When a child is born, they are not ruled by any limitations, and thereby, experience life being unattached to negativity. Then while growing up with parents who have tendencies to fear, they learn and adapt to living with similar outlooks.

That is exactly how the subconscious mind works. It is like an audio recording, which is going to play exactly what is recorded on it. The child's subconscious mind is transcribing the fears and limiting concepts from the surrounding environment onto a new program. As an adult, while watching news, reading fear-based articles, and watching violent movies on a consistent basis, the subconscious mind reinforces those destructive patterns.

Sadly, since subconscious programming influences your destiny, consistent exposure to negative messages diminish positive experiences. Remember, you are like a vessel; what you fill yourself with is what you will radiate. Fear can be compared with toxic and low-vibrational energy that emits pessimistic emotions. Additionally, being afraid is not fun. Not only can it manifest dreadful situations but also negatively affect your health and well-being.

Mistakes or Gifts?

One of the definitions of F.E.A.R. is False Evidence Appearing Real, but if you concentrate on it long enough, the sentiment may cease to be artificial. One realization that can help you overcome fears is the perspective that events occurring in your life happen for you, rather than to you.

Remember a tragic circumstance from the past and ask yourself a question: "Was it a disaster or an important lesson?" Looking back at my own experiences, I have come to realize that the past mistakes and misfortunes were actually stepping stones to the profound inner transformation. That is when I learned to stop fearing similar occurrences, as they were my gifts of awakening rather than tragic events.

Fears and Limiting Patterns

I would like to give you an example of my client, Katarina, who had a hard time enjoying life due to constant fears and worries. When I consulted her, she had just been hired for a new job with a high salary. Her car was very old, and she lived in an apartment with two roommates in a poor neighborhood. Despite the fact that her now-higher earnings could cover her moving to a new, beautiful place and buying a more reliable car, fear of losing her current job prevented Katarina from relishing an abundant and blissful life.

Katarina grew up in a very poor family, and there were times they could not afford basic needs. The poverty mentality and the fears of the family were so deeply imprinted in her subconscious mind that she could not possibly feel abundant. In order to transform those conditions, Katarina needed to shift the limiting beliefs, dissociate from the childhood perceptions, and implement new plentiful notions.

Recognize that fears do not serve your growth and success. How can you possibly experience the best life if you spend so much time worrying about the worst possible outcomes? Do you understand how much vital energy you are giving away? And what if those fears do manifest?

I know at the core of your being you don't seek those outcomes. Nevertheless, I asked Katarina to think about this for a few minutes: What if losing the job was exactly what needed to happen in order for the universe to gift her with an even more enjoyable and higher-paying job? For that reason, I recommended that, instead of worrying, Katarina should work on strengthening the abundance consciousness and surrender to the things that were out of her control.

This story illustrates the importance of learning to transcend the attachment to life's occurrences by focusing on feeling positive emotions and having ultimate trust. This way, you will stop disrupting the flow of divine synchronicities and instead invite miraculous experiences.

Fear of Rejection

One of the very common fears is fear of rejection. This fear has deep roots in our history. Long ago, when people lived together in large communities, being rejected would often lead to violent punishment, banishment, or even death. Some individuals are still carrying an imprint of the memories of the collective consciousness, while others feel the fear due to experiencing rejection and a lack of love in early childhood.

In order to eliminate fear of rejection, an individual should strengthen their self-image and return to a childlike state of bliss and innocence. Children are like animals; they are true to their personality and spirit, regardless of the pressure they are under. This is partly why they frequently excite everyone's interest and admiration.

Contrarily, the adults who inhibit and artificially orient their personality to be accepted by others are often rejected due to not being purely genuine. On a deep level, all of us are intuitive beings, which is why you may sense when someone's ulterior motive is to please or manipulate you.

Did you know that the secret of most successful leaders is the elimination of the fear of being rejected? The cause of many great innovations and new creations being developed was thanks to someone not being afraid to go against public opinion or to make a mistake.

Vincent van Gogh's paintings were misunderstood and not accepted by his generation, yet in the modern world, one of his paintings was sold for $82.5 million. In a similar instance, Martin Luther King Jr.'s message, at the time he lived, was not accepted by many people and was met with fierce opposition. Yet his desire to change the world was far greater than the fear of being rejected, and as a result, we even have a holiday to honor this great leader.

There are multiple examples of famous and successful people whose ideas were rejected by the majority, yet who, through their perseverance, created a great impact. For this reason, do not allow the fear of rejection to hold you back; instead let your talents and abilities bloom.

I would like to give you another example. A friend of mine, a painter, has never held an exhibition of his work and refuses to sell his paintings because of the fear of public opinion. The fear of rejection is immensely strong, impeding his talent and undermining the passion for showing his work to others. He would rather work in a shop as a salesperson than display his art.

It is such a limited and self-destructive way to live life when an individual doesn't use the potential, skills, and talents they were born with due to that limitation. Just imagine how much more you can bring into this world by simply eliminating the fear of rejection. There is always a possibility that some people will not accept and maybe even criticize you or your work. Conversely, by allowing those fears to take control over your life, you only sacrifice the stature of your accomplishments and the quality of your life.

Fear Is Selfish

Another example of how fear can negatively impact your life is evident in a client of mine, Ricardo, who happens to be a lawyer. His job entails speaking in front of a large audience. Each time he had to represent a client in court, his heart rate would go up and negative, fearful thoughts would attack his mind. Ricardo would imagine the worst possible outcome. The reason for it was very simple—a fear of rejection. Fear of public speaking is a very common fear. The life of a person who has to or wants to speak in public can be made much more difficult by giving in to this limitation.

To stop giving power to this fear, I advised Ricardo to imagine himself speaking in front of a large audience, yet instead of worrying, feeling excited and motivated to stand for justice and protection of his client's rights. I also advised him to answer the following question, "How can you really contribute to humanity when you only think about yourself in relation to other people's thoughts and opinions of you?"

Ricardo immediately realized how selfish he was in being absorbed by the fears while being fully responsible for the client's results. Once the life of the client was prioritized, the fears miraculously turned into excitement, the quality of his work improved significantly, and Ricardo's career took on a more positive momentum.

I learned this powerful skill while practicing the craft of acting. I had multiple auditions a week and felt exceedingly nervous. Once my acting teacher asked me, "Were you going to an audition or to an opportunity to perform the task the scene? Were you going there to save your daughter, who according to the script was in danger, or were you going there to please a casting director?" When I clarified my goal, the fears turned into an enthusiasm and passion for the right purpose.

Fear and Relationships

My client Becky had experienced many rejections in past relationships and, in order to avoid similar outcomes, decided to become socially isolated. Consequently, she found herself lonely most of the time. This is an example of a fear created in early childhood due to lack of love and attention. As I mentioned earlier, when a child doesn't receive enough deep affection, their brain may create a program in which rejection becomes a familiar pattern.

This pattern of attracting familiar but detrimental situations is commonly referred to as "repetition compulsion." It is a psychological phenomenon where individuals unconsciously seek out and recreate familiar dynamics, even if those dynamics are harmful or negative.

The brain's attempt to create a program of familiar patterns is a survival mechanism. In childhood, when love and attention are lacking, the brain adapts to this environment by creating patterns that help the child make sense of their experiences. However, these patterns can become deeply ingrained and continue to influence an individual's choices and behaviors into adulthood.

Becky's childhood experiences shed light on the origins of her fear and isolation. Growing up in a large family with parents who were constantly working and not spending quality time with their children resulted in Becky not receiving the love and attention she needed. Additionally, being ridiculed by her classmates for her speech difficulties further contributed to her sense of unworthiness.

As Becky grew older, she developed a strong drive to prove her worthiness to others and herself. This drive led her to achieve wealth and status. Despite being successful, nevertheless, Becky still carried deep-seated emptiness, limiting beliefs, and fears. Her fear of public gatherings was a clear manifestation of those underlying insecurities and lack of self-love.

I advised Becky to work on the subconscious programming and eliminate the negative beliefs that were ingrained in her from past experiences. By actively working on altering the negative self-image and cultivating self-love and self-acceptance, Becky gradually eliminated the fears and insecurities. As she began to see her own beauty and magnificence, her confidence grew, and she became open to attending public events and attracting meaningful connections in her life.

Remember, building a strong and powerful relationship with oneself is the foundation for healthy connections with others. When you have a solid sense of self-worth and self-love, you eradicate the fear of rejection and are less likely to seek validation and approval from external sources. Instead, you can engage in relationships from a place of authenticity and emotional well-being.

Fears and Affirmations

You can compare fears with negative habits, which you can now transform into positive ones. If all your life you have lived in fear, be gentle with yourself; your mind may still have a tendency to attract what is familiar. To implement new constructive patterns, start practicing affirmations.

For example, if you are afraid of public speaking or being in public gatherings, consistently say to yourself expressions like these: "I absolutely love speaking in front of a large audience. I feel exceptionally confident, and I radiate my best qualities while in any public gathering. I am lovable and great at my craft."

While your thoughts have a profound effect on the subconscious, your feelings have an even more powerful one. While saying affirmations, feel them as if they are already a part of you. Sing them if you would like—and remember, repetition is the key to reprogramming your mind.

Fears and Visualization

Another effective practice to transform patterns of fear is visualization. Your mind truly doesn't know the difference between real and imagined circumstances. Thereby, the more you envision your ideal outcomes, the faster they can be realized.

For instance, if you are afraid of flying, close your eyes for a few minutes several times a day and imagine yourself being happy and peaceful while flying. By doing so consistently, you are creating a new pattern in your brain, which, with enough practice, will win over the limiting one.

Canceling Fears

When you feel stuck in fearful thoughts, command your mind: CANCEL, CANCEL, CANCEL. You are not always in complete control of the kind of thoughts entering your consciousness. Nonetheless, with enough practice and dedication, you can attain total mastery of the kind of thoughts you allow into your heart.

At certain moments, you simply have fearful and negative thoughts, and those may not always be yours. What I mean is, occasionally, you may sense the fears and negativity of others, the environment, or the media.

Saying the word CANCEL stops those thoughts from influencing your reality by not allowing the subconscious mind to accept those stories, or by simply canceling them out. The mind is a brilliant tool, and by saying "stop" or "cancel," you are able to reject negativity and block the limiting subconscious blueprint.

Any time you feel fearful and negative thoughts, ask yourself a question: "Is this the experience I truly wish to manifest?" If the answer is no, please CANCEL those ideas, as life is too magnificent to continuously attract atrocious events.

MASTERING YOUR MIND

In order to learn how to master fears, you should learn to quiet your mind. Throughout this book I mention multiple times the importance of a still mind because a mind that is constantly thinking is akin to a person running a marathon without taking a break. How exhausting would that be? For this reason, mastering stillness is crucial to winning your inner state.

One of the quickest and simplest methods to learn how to quiet the mind is to become aware of your breathing. Deep breathing makes it harder to have busy, distracting thoughts because it allows you to become detached from your mind and enter a surrendered state.

Nevertheless, deep breathing is probably not something you were taught in school, and that is why in order to turn it into a new habit, you should practice it on a daily basis. Begin with just a few deep breaths during the day, and eventually increase the time spent on this powerful practice.

As I mentioned earlier, you can also add feelings to this exercise such as love or gratitude. Imagine a beautiful sparkling light filled with those positive emotions entering you with each breath and charging your heart with this salubrious energy. After doing this exercise, start practicing living in that state, even just for brief moments at first.

The more you do so, the stronger and more natural it will become. You'll find that love and gratitude become your default emotional state, and that they have the potential to overpower any fearful thoughts that arise. So, embrace this exercise and let it become a cornerstone of your well-being. I will cover the practice of stillness in more detail in the forthcoming chapter, "The Power of Being Present."

In conclusion, remember, the voice in your head that speaks fears is actually there to protect you. Once you learn to silence this voice while in safe situations, you will stop creating unnecessary anxiety and unfavorable experiences.

Remember, you hold the power to overcome fears by challenging negative thoughts and questioning their truthfulness. Additionally, implementing visualization and affirmation practices is highly beneficial in achieving favorable outcomes. In some instances, it is essential to cancel out negative thoughts in order to eliminate their influence on the subconscious.

Lastly, tame your mind by learning to be still to eradicate the harmful effect of fearful thoughts on your overall well-being. You are given this lifetime to live once. Why create negative experiences?

PART IV
AWAKEN LOVE WITHIN

CHAPTER 10

THE POWER OF SELF-LOVE

"When you love yourself, you become a magnet for all of your heart's desires."

Self-love is one of the fastest paths to inner transformation. Loving yourself doesn't mean narcissism; it means total acceptance of yourself and all of your past choices. Complete acceptance implies that you stop criticizing yourself and, instead, reinforce encouraging and loving notions.

The subject of self-love is not something that is taught in schools; that is why many people on this planet neither practice it nor understand its importance. Innumerable individuals assume that self-criticism is a normal part of their existence. Nevertheless, it is detrimental to your growth and the development of your full potential.

Let's envision a beautiful garden with many different flowers, plants, and trees. In order for this garden to flourish and bloom, you must water it and fertilize it with necessary nutrients.

As well, you should remove weeds, which stunt the growth of healthy plants. Loving and supportive words toward yourself can be compared to the water and nutrients that are influencing you to grow and bloom. Self-criticism, on the other hand, is like weeds that prevent you from evolving.

Master Self-Love?

To master self-love means you should start treating yourself as though you were your own child or someone you love. The majority of parents would give unconditional love to their own children, which is akin to how you should treat yourself. The process may not be a miraculous overnight event, but a shift in your attitude that will completely change your life.

Have you ever criticized yourself for the wrong choices you made in the past? Some individuals have a tendency to treat other people better than they treat themselves. If you had a friend, for example, who often criticized you, you would probably have an urge to protect yourself. When was the last time you protected yourself from your own criticism?

Many conflicts and misunderstandings arise from a lack of self-love. When you do not know how to love yourself and when the relationship with yourself is shallow, you become vulnerable and easily emotionally disturbed. In other words, no one can bring you pain. Others can only awaken what is already inside of you.

Additionally, self-love shifts your perception of how you view others. You start seeing those who misbehave toward you with the eyes of love. You see their wounded heart rather than their negative intention. While it is important not to take it personally when people lash out at you, it is still essential to protect yourself in the process; for this is also a part of loving yourself.

SELF-LOVE AND MENTAL HEALTH

Did you know that the many mental conditions such as clinical depression, obsessive compulsive disorder, and bipolar disorder, at their root, be traced to a lack of self-love? I myself went through a phase in which I endured a mental health crisis due to the loss of my parents and the consistent abuse I received in my childhood.

When I was in my early twenties, the pain was strong and, honestly, intolerable. That is when I asked for help from a medical psychologist who diagnosed me with bipolar disorder and referred me to a psychiatrist to get some medication. In spite of that, some deep voice within stopped me from following her advice.

I was lucky enough to meet an incredible hypnotherapist, Brian Green, who believed in my healing and disagreed with the previous doctor`s diagnosis. Within a few sessions, my pain was no longer intolerable, and a new emerging hope in complete emotional mastery had been awakened. What I later realized was this: that exact pain was actually the driving force toward my path of transformation.

I believe, nevertheless, that as a collective consciousness, we should not wait for life to give us intense struggle to awaken to the light, and we should not settle for the path that appears easy, but which truly can bring more harm than you can even realize. It seems so simple for many people to drug themselves with pharmaceuticals when they are diagnosed with these mental diseases instead of learning to create a loving and nurturing relationship with oneself. I strongly believe that self-love is truly a key to healthy emotional and mental health.

This subject is so very close to my heart, and it is my mission to bring awareness to this pivotal element of life. I was diagnosed with bipolar disorder, and I have had many clients who have been affected by similar issues. Fortunately, compared to those who chose a path of pharmaceutical rehabilitation, my clients and I successfully eliminated all the symptoms with the power of self-love.

The reason I believe that a multitude of mental illnesses come from a lack of self-love is, when you deny your own magnificence, the harsh and critical words toward yourself can make you feel insane.

I don't deny the fact that there are people who have serious mental conditions that require actual medical involvement. For those individuals, my recommendation is to work on self-love and self-acceptance simultaneously. Bipolar disorder, for example, is associated with episodes of mood swings ranging from depressive to manic. It can be caused by genetics, environment, and altered brain chemistry. I can't argue completely against such a diagnosis.

What I would like to say, though, is this: when I was in my early teenage years, I experienced severe mood swings. At that time, along with hypnotherapy, I tapped into my heart for answers. What I learned was that the strong anger, pain, and depression were coming due to endless and incessant self-criticism.

And the more I fell in love with me and learned to accept myself with all my imperfections, the faster those mood swings vanished, as I stopped torturing myself in my own mind. I believe this realization awakened my inner healing and removed the unbearable symptoms that the doctors readily had called bipolar disorder.

What I also realized on my journey to self-love is that when you become a victor instead of letting yourself feel victimized, you stop being ignorant of the conditions and circumstances that your inner state reflects. And when you learn to perceive the challenges in your life as your greatest teacher, you rise above all limitations.

SELF-LOVE AND YOUR CHOICES

Did you know that a lack of self-love negatively influences the choices you make in life? When you do not love yourself, your own self-defeating thoughts can lead you to make decisions that project dissatisfaction in life.

Remember Dr. Emoto`s water-based experiment that I mentioned earlier, which reveals the power of this process? The water infused with positive affirmations resulted in ice crystals that were far more symmetrical and aesthetically pleasing, while the water infused with negative affirmations formed ice crystals that were discolored and fragmented.

If you criticize and put yourself down, you change your frequencies just like water changes its structure, and as a result, you become blind to healthy opportunities. Instead, you begin experiencing turmoil, which you yourself choose unconsciously.

SELF-LOVE AND SUCCESS

Success and self-love come hand in hand. Loving yourself is another expression of a deep-seated positive belief in oneself. Self-love means having a high regard for your own well-being which assists you in making powerful choices. When you love yourself, you feel worthy of success and expand your possibilities.

There are some people who achieve enormous success while not loving themselves. They are usually driven toward their desires in order to prove themselves to others. A lack of self-love pushes them to become successful so that others begin to admire them.

Yet, it never works. When an individual does not feel enough, any sort of achievement will fall short of truly satisfying them. And they will soon realize that love received from the outside world does not fill the empty gap within.

Certainly, the admiration of success garnered from others will bring some passing pleasure but not fulfill this individual for long. Often those who achieve massive success without loving themselves and who come to realize it was not the cure for their emptiness turn to self-destructive behaviors, such as heavy addictions.

Self-Love and Addictions

Addictions such as excessive drinking, smoking, drug abuse, and any others are often the result of not loving oneself. When you love yourself, you begin admiring and caring for every part of you. Subsequently, your body will naturally begin rejecting and disliking substances that are not good for you and become your greatest guide without the need for rigid rules and diets.

Furthermore, addictive substances are often taken to fill the emptiness and sadness in one's heart. When you love yourself, on the contrary, you are whole and complete, and the need for anything else to make you feel better disappears because you are already living in your best state.

Addictions are not limited to substances only; people find crutches in all sorts of vices. One such example is acquiring material possessions. Some people start believing that their value will increase if they acquire more things.

Those individuals collect luxury cars, homes, and accessories, and yet deep inside, they still feel incomplete because, remember, the world of material objects will not add much to a feeling of wholeness within. Self-love, in contrast, will give birth to feelings of richness and fulfillment in one's heart, which will manifest as an abundant life.

SELF-LOVE AND RELATIONSHIPS

The other benefit of loving yourself is that other people will start responding toward you with more love, admiration, and respect. Every relationship in your life is simply a mirror of the relationship with yourself. It is hard to hear sometimes, yet it is an undeniable truth. All the connections suffer when you do not know how to love yourself.

Conversely, when you master this vital relationship with yourself, your frequency rises, and you attract a partner, a friend, or a business associate on similar vibrations, and instead of creating consistent drama, you facilitate harmony.

When you love yourself, you stop being a victim and accusing others of their bad choices. You no longer take the actions of others personally, and instead of going into conflict, you take their actions as a way to go deeper within and transform your own self further.

Loving yourself also means finding harmony and peace in your own company. How many people believe that some other person will make them happy? It never works. Until you create a nurturing connection with yourself, stepping into a relationship with another may come from the need to be loved or from the unconscious necessity to feel more complete. Understand that the other person can never complete you, and those relationships often fail. That is the reason why the most effortless path to a fulfilling connection is acceptance and love of yourself.

Let's return to the analogy of the garden. Imagine a beautiful rose that is ready to grow and bloom. Unfortunately, weeds are absorbing her nutrients and drinking her water. The rose does receive the love from the sun, but the weeds in the earth do not allow her to be healthy and blossom to the fullest.

You are a beautiful rose. The lack of self-love and limiting beliefs are the weeds, and the sun is the unconditional love from Higher Consciousness. And in order for you to reach the highest potential, it is essential to eliminate the limiting patterns at their roots.

Imagine how much you can give to your loved ones and the world when you master self-love! You radiate what you fill yourself with. If you are dominated by pain and resentment, that is what you project on others. When you are governed by love, that is exactly what shines through you.

Love Is a Powerful Medicine

Did you know that a lack of self-love can lead to all kinds of illnesses? As previously discussed, the example of Louise Hay rectifying her health with the power of self-love is a vivid reminder of the importance of this essential relationship with oneself. With the power of self-love and self-acceptance, she was able to heal cancer.

If you still doubt the potential of this internal connection, try it out for yourself. If you suffer from any chronic pain or disease, begin loving yourself and pay close attention to the part of the body that is hurting. Send all your love into that area and remain open to the possibility of miraculous healing.

Each area of your body is associated with a specific area of your life. For instance, if you have problems with the neck, it is likely directly related with your throat chakra, which is the area of communication and self-expression. Therefore, begin by accepting and admiring what you have to say.

If you often question yourself in hindsight, remember that everything you ever said, so long as it was rooted in honesty and good intention, in all probability, needed to be expressed. In the past, I often had neck problems and suffered from a chronic sore throat. When I accepted myself and my self-expression, the conditions miraculously improved.

If you have problems with the stomach, then you probably have problems with self-identity and self-confidence, as this area is correlated with the solar plexus chakra. As I mentioned earlier, not loving yourself develops negative self-esteem. Thus, learn to love yourself and be amazed by naturally occurring healing.

Problems with the bladder are most commonly associated with imbalance in the area of sexuality, creativity, and bliss. To strengthen this area, begin with a full and complete love and acceptance of your body and your sexual organs. So many people feel shame about that part of themselves. Realize that shame only leads to stagnation in this area. Self-love and acceptance, on the other hand, will set you free from suffering and will influence a healthier and much more enjoyable life.

If you experience constant headaches or problems with your head, you must be living too much in the mind and thinking too many negative thoughts. In order to transform this condition, become devoted to loving yourself by learning to shift the attention to your heart and radiate love and self-acceptance.

I have to tell you that when I didn't know how to love myself, I had all kinds of illnesses, despite the fact that I was very young. I would go from one doctor to another only to discover another ailment. When I fell in love with me and began living in a constant state of love and acceptance, an optimal well-being prevailed.

Consequently, in order to strengthen your immune system, improve overall health, increase energy level, and eliminate physical ailments, realize that loving and kind thoughts, total unconditional love, and a complete approval of yourself are your best medicine.

Self-Love and Beauty

When you start loving yourself, you blossom like a beautiful flower. The flowers that get the most admiration flourish and bloom longer and spread more aromas. When you start loving yourself unconditionally, many people in your surroundings will notice it. When you stop seeing your imperfections as negative qualities, they can instantly turn into your greatest strengths.

Appearance and beauty are highly subjective topics as everyone has their own unique taste. Many times, my clients have asked me, "How can I ever love myself if I am unattractive and my body is far from perfect?" There are only two answers to this question. You can choose to put emphasis on the self-imposed imperfections and make them more noticeable to others, or you can choose to fall in love with every part of yourself and transform them into a more attractive version.

Have you ever met a person who was not very attractive according to some societal standards, yet other people were magnetically drawn to them? It is because their inner beauty and magnetism radiate so brightly that they outshine the outer appearance.

I would like to give an example. A few years ago, I had a client, Anna, who is extremely beautiful. In her conversations, however, Anna was self-critical about her appearance. She called her nose a "potato" and referred to her legs as "chicken legs." But that was quite contrary to what I saw. This beautiful lady could have been the cover girl on any fashion magazine and won a best body competition. Unfortunately, Anna was not able to see her own beauty.

In addition to being exceptionally attractive, Anna was highly intelligent and talented. Sadly, she found herself constantly rejected and heartbroken. At the time we met, she had recently gone through a painful breakup. Her ex-boyfriend consistently played on her insecurities and verbally reminded Anna of her perceived physical flaws.

This story illustrates how other people's behavior toward you is a reflection of your relationship with yourself. Other people are merely mirrors of that reflection. If Anna had loved her appearance, she would not have attracted a verbally abusive partner but rather someone capable of seeing her beauty. This story also educates us that physical attributes may be a basis for an initial impression but not a major component in a lasting perception.

Remember, when you love yourself, you send loving, beautiful thoughts about yourself to others. We are all deeply connected. You emit your thoughts to others as though you have invisible antennas.

I knew a woman, named Lily, who was preparing for a very important business interview. She would close her eyes for a few minutes a day and send those imaginary people the thoughts about her best qualities. Additionally, she radiated unconditional love toward herself. Lily was almost in tears of bliss when she told me her story. "Not only did the meeting go extremely well but I also received compliments on the exact traits of my personality I was focusing on and loving the most."

STEPS TO LOVE YOURSELF

1. Stop any self-criticism.

When you make a wrong choice, do you immediately start criticizing yourself? Understand that you are powerful enough to change your thoughts, and remember, it is just a matter of habit. You become excellent at any skill you implement consistently.

When self-criticizing thoughts enter your mind, acknowledge them, but replace them with more positive and uplifting ones. Of course, it may seem unnatural at first since it is a new habit. The more you practice this new way of being, nevertheless, the more effortless and enjoyable it will become.

2. Start practicing affirmations with your heart.

It is not easy to shift your thoughts at first because your beliefs are rooted deeply in the subconscious mind. That is why when most people decide to change their beliefs and habits, they quit within the first two weeks.

According to various studies, it is necessary to keep practicing new skills for at least twenty-one days to transform a pattern on the subconscious level. But keep in mind, it is a continuous process since personal transformation is a perpetual process of self-improvement.

Affirmations are a very powerful practice to refine the beliefs you have about yourself. And as I stated earlier, the reason why affirmations fail to work in some cases is that they are often performed in the wrong way. They should be felt in your heart rather than simply said. For example, merely voicing positive statements without feeling them makes them less likely to reach the subconscious mind. Conversely, by believing in your heart and with every cell of the body whatever you are saying, a new positive pattern will be born.

Self-love affirmations

- I love you just the way you are.
- I am so very beautiful inside and out.
- I am magnificent and powerful.
- I love you and forgive you.

- I am lovable and I deserve love.
- I am special and I am gifted.
- I deserve to be loved.
- I create a loving relationship with myself.

3. Start practicing self-love in actions.

What actions are you willing to take to start loving yourself? As previously mentioned, so many people's words don't align with their actions. When you master your inner monologues while not changing behavioral patterns, you do not really achieve the desired results.

If you stop criticizing and begin praising yourself instead, yet you do not rest enough, continue eating junk food, smoking cigarettes, and staying in abusive relationships, your behavior is contradicting the new positive self-image. In this scenario, you only changed the pattern of thoughts, not the actual behavior. To start loving yourself in actions, begin by answering the following questions:

A) Do I carve out quality time with myself?
B) Do the people in my close circle treat me with love and respect?
C) Do I reward myself with simple pleasures?
D) Do I rest enough?
E) Do I consume a healthy diet?
F) Is it easy for me to accept compliments?
G) Do I praise even my smallest accomplishments?
H) Do I believe I deserve to experience the best life?

If the answer to some of these questions is no, immediately make the necessary changes. You are capable enough to do that. *If you ever doubt that you are a powerful creator, realize that whatever circumstances you are experiencing right now were created by you.*

4. Continue working on your subconscious beliefs.

Understand that lack of self-love is the outcome of a deeply rooted subconscious belief such as "I am not enough," "Something is wrong with me," or "I am unlovable." By changing your thoughts and feelings, you will eventually create new positive beliefs.

Remember, though, those limitations were created at the subconscious level, and transforming them while working directly with your subconscious mind will be so much more effective. In the earlier chapter "Identifying and Removing Subconscious Beliefs," I provided step-by-step instructions to alter similar negative patterns.

5. Become aware of your circle of influence.

It happens sometimes that you outgrow those around you, and in some cases even cause resentment in relation to your inner growth and success. A powerful quote from Jack Canfield, an American author and motivational speaker, provides us with a powerful insight: "You become like the people you spend the most time with." When you begin loving yourself, and some of the closest people in your life do not awaken to the same truth, those individuals may not support your growth and, instead, actually slow you down.

You are never static: you are moving either forward or backward. Let's say, during a conversation, you would like to share newly formed positive insights, while your so-called friends continue spreading negativity. You certainly can attempt to help those around you to change. You should not, however, gravitate toward those who are resenting and devaluing your advice. Otherwise, it will be challenging to evolve to the next level.

It may be a painful and unpleasant experience to put an end to certain relationships at first, yet this act will open the doors for new positive and high-vibrational people to enter your life. Realize that it is much easier to progress when those closest to you are ready for new, more powerful ways to experience life.

6. Forgive yourself and others.

Some people have a hard time releasing past mistakes and wrong choices. Realize that forgiveness frees you from unconsciously held limitations. What I have noticed is that some of my clients claimed they forgave and released their past, yet in conversations, I noticed they had a hard time speaking kindly about those experiences.

This is not true forgiveness. If you have authentically forgiven someone or yourself, all that should remain is acceptance and love. Specifically, when you truly release the pain, it becomes easy to speak about the event or the person and refer to the experience as a blessing rather than an unpleasant occurrence.

In conclusion, self-love is an essential quality in order to create a life of abundance, fulfillment, and wellness. When you love yourself, you reflect harmonious relationships and high-vibrational healing energy into the world. To master self-love, you must stop criticizing yourself and instead begin treating yourself as someone you love dearly.

Loving yourself also means shifting self-destructive behaviors, poor eating habits, and corrosive influences. Remember how you felt when you were in love with someone. You felt so alive and enriched by life. Why not fall in love with yourself and create magic daily?

CHAPTER 11
SACRED SPACE OF YOUR HEART

"A coherent and loving heart is the key to radiant health and a fulfilled life."

Your heart is more than an essential organ that pumps blood. As a matter of fact, your heart emits electrical signals, which are, on average, sixty to one hundred times stronger than those of the brain, and a magnetic field, which is up to five hundred times stronger as well.

In 1991, pioneer researcher J. Andrew Armour, MD, PhD, discovered that the heart has approximately forty thousand neurons. Not nerves, but actual *neurons*—cells that transmit information throughout the body, control glands, and are collectively capable of memory, reasoning, and even *thoughts*.

In ancient Egypt, when a pharaoh or another person of great importance or wealth died, their body was preserved through mummification. As part of this process, many of the vital organs were removed, as they are generally the first to decompose, and the stomach, intestines, lungs, and liver were placed into special decorative containers known as canopic jars. The heart, interestingly, was considered the seat of both feeling *and* intelligence, and thus, was left in the body to help guide the deceased into the afterlife. The brain was considered largely useless and tossed aside.

Heart Abilities

According to scientist and author Gregg Braden, recent studies of heart tissue suggest that your heart is capable of living and pumping for three hundred years or more. Yet heart failure remains the leading cause of death, according to the World Health Organization.

In the context of what I now understand about this incredible organ and its capabilities, it would not be unreasonable to assume that most heart diseases are, at their roots, heart dis-ease. To say it differently, stress, suffering, and any other negative emotions experienced in the heart shorten our life span. It is, therefore, more than just a figure of speech to say that our society is indeed dying of broken hearts.

There is much talk in professional athletic circles about muscle memory—yet few stop to consider the importance of *heart* memory, which, do not forget, is also a muscle. Yes, just like a muscle learns through repetitive actions, so too does the heart learn to repeat (or, rather, re-feel) the emotions that you experience most often. That is also where the lingering energy from deep-seated traumas is generally stored. And if left untreated, over time, it begins to fester.

Positive Emotions

If this hasn`t yet demonstrated the power and importance of positive thinking and feeling positive emotions for you, let`s consider one more amazing medical fact: simply shifting your emotions from negative to positive, within seconds, causes over 1,400 different chemicals to be released into your bloodstream.

Among these is dehydroepiandrosterone, or DHEA, a naturally occurring steroid from which important hormones such as testosterone and estrogen are made. And, in case you did not know, these are among the chief ways one's biological age (as opposed to chronological age) can be measured. So, quite literally, feeling good helps you stay young.

Wellness vs. Illness

You see, when you are stressed or upset, your body releases hormones such as adrenaline and cortisol. These are responsible for the "fight or flight" response, and they are meant for short-lasting emergency situations (such as escaping from a shark), and not as an everyday function.

In the short term, these hormones can help elevate your heart rate and breathing and prepare your muscles for action. Prolonged exposure, contrariwise, can lead to conditions such as depression or anxiety, headaches, memory and concentration issues, poor digestion, insomnia, high blood sugar, weight gain, heart disease, and other serious illnesses. In other words, many of the common signs of aging.

Cortisol, the stress hormone, breaks down DHEA. So, the more cortisol you have in your system, the less freely available DHEA you will have. And, to make matters worse, multiple studies have shown that taking DHEA supplements does absolutely nothing to affect DHEA levels in the blood. The *only* reliable way to make more DHEA is by feeling good.

Some researchers also demonstrated that loving touch helps increase DHEA production. What is also important to know is that

DHEA can actually break down the stress hormone cortisol, which as I mentioned earlier can be the cause of serious health issues.

THE HEART'S INTELLIGENCE

So, what are some of the ways you can shift your mood and help these wonderful chemical reactions to occur? It starts with getting out of your head and back into your heart. Many people believe that emotional reactions come solely from the brain. It is true that they do without proper practice, as many individuals tend to identify with every thought that crosses their mind.

When you start living from a place of a coherent heart, nonetheless, you lessen the negative influence of the mind. Previously I mentioned that your mind can receive messages from outside sources without even being aware of it. The good news is that when you are grounded in love and appreciation in your heart, those messages lose their influence on your feelings.

Understand that the mind is an incredibly powerful tool, yet it can trick you into believing that your inner monologues define who you are. It is very easy to get lost in your own thoughts and create unnecessary stress. *Your heart, on the other hand, is your sole connection to inner peace.*

MIND VS. HEART

Remember, the mind easily assigns meaning to the events that occur in your life. Let's say you just had a disagreement with someone. Your mind may create all kinds of stories involving negative emotions such as blame, guilt, or anger.

Conversely, if you are attuned to the love frequency of your heart, it is much easier to feel love and compassion, and the interpretation of the situation tends to be much more positive.

Heart and Intuition

When you learn to experience love in your heart on a consistent basis, you become not only more successful, healthier, and fulfilled but also more intuitive. I believe that you must tap into the heart's intelligence in order to interpret intuitive messages. And when trained properly, the heart has much more potential for being an intuitive guiding force than the brain.

Now you may understand the famous Albert Einstein quote, "The intuitive mind is a sacred gift, and the rational mind is a faithful servant. We have created a society that honors the servant and has forgotten the gift." I know that Einstein refers to the intuitive mind. I have noticed, however, that intuitive messages may flow through the mind, yet the one who can interpret them is the one who has fully embraced their heart.

That is why the key to fulfillment and success is experiencing life from a healthy and coherent heart while using the brain when it is necessary. This way, you will always be divinely guided to make the choices that will assist you in effortlessly creating abundance in every area. That is also when you will stop being a servant of your own brain, which frequently has a hard time resting, enjoying life, and simply relaxing.

Sacred Heart Exercise

Take three deep breaths. Now take another breath and feel a beautiful pink or golden light flowing through your heart. Fill your heart with the emotions of love and appreciation. If it feels challenging to experience these powerful emotions, remember a past event or a moment that awakened those feelings and relive them.

The more frequently you practice this exercise, the faster you will excel at it. The more you tune in to this powerful state, the easier it will be to achieve inner peace and happiness and go through life's challenges with ease and grace.

Conscious Living

When your attention is fully in your heart, that is when it is possible to experience unconditional love for yourself and for others. That is when miracles start taking place, leading to a spectacular journey.

Imagine waking up every day feeling only love and gratitude, feeling a return to childlike innocence and satiety, leading to a memory of who you truly are, which is a being of pure light and consciousness.

All of this happens while living in the sacred space of the heart, because within the heart is consciousness, and being fully conscious is the realization of oneness.

Heart and Success

Positive thinking is surely a powerful skill, yet feeling positive is so much more effective. I am convinced that when you feel abundant, you become an effortless manifestor. When you feel something in your heart fully, you experience a sense of wholeness and trust.

Furthermore, if you would like to realize the career you love, feel yourself as a person who is already successful in this field. Learn to live this feeling in your heart as often as possible and realize your aspirations as a result.

It is believed by some individuals that you must work hard to be successful. I believe that when you are attuned to the love and appreciation frequency of your heart, the work you choose becomes your biggest passion, and abundance follows as a result.

That is when the journey becomes astonishing, and you cease creating challenges. The solutions to complications come more easily as well since you no longer waste your time on unnecessary negative stories of your mind. In this state, you become a wellspring of prosperity, joy, and contentment.

Love Heals

In her book *A Return to Love* (1992), American author Marianne Williamson mentions a very powerful story. An experiment was done with rabbits that were tested using a drug that had side effects. All the rabbits experienced severe effects, except one.

What the researchers later found out was that the animal that had no side effects was hugged and given love by a boy who was feeding him. The boy was so in love with the rabbit that he would spend all his free time with him.

The healing power of love is enormous, and only ignorance of this essential truth leads to unhappiness, disease, and general dissatisfaction. I believe that the most efficacious way to heal yourself and create a positive impact in the world is by becoming aware of the power of love and learning to experience life with optimistic emotions.

In conclusion, your heart is a conduit for the life that is intended for you to manifest. Experiencing life from the sacred space of your heart will promote a lasting ability to control your emotions, enhanced well-being, and a stronger sense of intuition. This powerful state will shed away unnecessary stress and turmoil and assist you in creating a life of abundance and bliss.

CHAPTER 12

CREATE A FULFILLING RELATIONSHIP

"A fulfilling relationship is a reflection of a fulfilled heart."

Being in love is one of the most beautiful and powerful states a person can ever experience. Additionally, an intimate relationship is probably the fastest way to grow and evolve, since your partner can often bring to the surface the blocks and limiting patterns that are hiding deep within you.

Unfortunately, not every couple is able to work through the challenges and sustain harmony and passion throughout the years. An unfulfilling relationship can lead to frustration and general dissatisfaction in life, and in some cases, even severe pain, or depression. The question then arises, "How can you sustain the first stages of love and divine bliss and transform any relationship from drama to inspiration?"

Is Separation Always a Solution?

In modern times, the divorce rate is very high. For example, the U.S. has the third-highest divorce rate in the world, while the Maldives and Belarus have even higher numbers. One of the reasons for this is that many people at the present time consider separation a common solution to marital problems. At the time my grandmother and grandfather were born, in the early twentieth century, divorce was not a common way to end a relationship, and many couples lived together their whole lives.

It doesn't mean those couples didn't encounter any challenges. It simply means that they were willing to put more effort and work in to save their relationship, as each partner perceived it as a sacred and meaningful connection in their life.

The benefit of staying together, however, doesn't apply to all couples. There are cases when two partners are not the best match for each other's growth and evolution, and in this circumstance, a separation can be a liberating experience. Also, life is a beautiful and magnificent school, which may bring you multiple partners as your teachers, before you engage in a more serious commitment such as marriage and children.

The Absence of a Relationship

There are also those individuals in modern times who experience challenges manifesting a relationship in the first place. If this is you, ask yourself a question: "What do I believe deep inside about love?"

I have met numerous clients undergoing similar conditions who were governed by the belief "I am not lovable" or "love is not possible in my world." The reason for this belief could be a lack of affection from parents or a dysfunctional family in early childhood in which a child creates a distorted view of relationships.

There are also those individuals who are not ready for a commitment at this moment. It is absolutely fine, as a season of solitude can be a great time for self-reflection and personal development. I do believe, though, that love and romance are an essential part of anyone's journey, so preparing for this vital step is highly beneficial.

Inner Work and Relationships

For those of you who are already in a relationship and are looking to improve it, it is essential to begin with yourself. Many couples tend to blame each other for dysfunctional behavior toward one another, without realizing that change must come from within. That is why constantly attempting to mold your partner just never works.

When you heal your internal limitations, your partner's behavior will reflect the new healthy state. Yet if you are governed by pain, your significant other will simply help you bring it to the surface. Realize that drama and conflict in a relationship arise from unresolved wounds inflicted in the past, and until those are healed, a partner in a relationship may change, but the conflicts are likely to remain.

Consequently, behind every successful relationship, there is work and inner transformation. An intimate relationship can be compared to a beautiful rose bush. When you water and fertilize it, the plant grows into its strongest and most beautiful form. In a relationship, when you and your partner invest time and effort in consistent inner growth, and are willing to compromise and learn new skills, just like the rose, together you will grow and strengthen your roots.

COMMUNICATION AND RELATIONSHIPS

What is one of the biggest challenges many couples face in any relationship? It is a misunderstanding, which is often caused by an inability to communicate clearly. This is likely due to the fact that it is just so much easier to make assumptions rather than hold honest and vulnerable discussions.

If what I just said relates closely to you, ask yourself the following questions: How often do I ask my partner to clarify what they really mean? When was the last time I had a sincere conversation? Realize that assumptions are frequently your mental filter's interpretation of your partner's behavior, rather than pure facts. And negative assumptions frequently lead to conflicts and drama in a relationship, while clear communication develops closeness and trust.

To communicate clearly means learning to be authentic and losing the fear of being judged. This is why self-love and self-acceptance are the foundation of a fulfilling relationship. It is common that, in some moments, you may feel hurt by certain words and behaviors of your partner. Instead of holding the bitterness, reveal how you truly feel about it in a gentle and polite way. In most cases, your partner's intention is not to hurt you, and they may not even be aware of your pain and suffering. That is why, instead of automatically viewing the situation as a conflict, consider it an opportunity to learn more about your companion's point of view.

By sharing your feelings, you allow your partner to become aware of the patterns you are working on, and as a team, you can heal them with so much less effort. Contrarily, when you do not explain what upsets you and instead express anger or other negative emotions, not only do you prevent the relationship from evolving but also negatively influence your growth, success, and quality of life.

The Languages of Relationships

A lot of times a couple may not realize their core values. For example, a wife who is highly feminine requires nurturing in order to feel loved. A husband who is highly career-oriented and a sole provider needs to feel appreciated for his efforts. Without a clear understanding, this connection may suffer.

What can happen in this situation is that the husband assumes that he gives love through dedicated work, yet the wife may feel abandoned and alone because her needs for deep love and affection are not being met. So instead of admiring her partner's work ethic, she may actually criticize this quality and perceive it as an obstacle.

By way of illustration, a friend of mine, Anna, complained that her husband didn't spend enough time with her and began resenting his work. When Anna and Alex were dating, she was working from 8 a.m. to 5 p.m. every day. During her pregnancy, she took maternity leave. Alex started working twice as much to give their newborn daughter the best possible life.

While Alex spent all his precious time creating a financial future for the growing family, Anna felt worried and unsatisfied. Due to an enormous amount of work, Alex felt tired and had hardly any energy to nurture or spend any quality time with his pregnant wife.

For days, Anna was sad and worried while hiding her true feelings about the situation until one day she could no longer take it. Alex arrived home from work and her emotions erupted, which led to a huge argument. The conflict could have been resolved much more smoothly if Anna had voiced her concerns earlier and Alex had explained the reason for his absence.

When Anna and Alex finally had an honest conversation, she confessed she felt an even deeper love for him for the drive to support their child. Anna also expressed a deeply felt trust in knowing that she could rely on her husband more than ever before. In return, Alex felt appreciated and touched and promised to make a concerted effort to spend quality time with Anna. Honesty and vulnerability strengthened their bond and awakened a new level of connection and intimacy in their relationship.

Similar situations occur due to how commonplace it is for some individuals to withhold their emotions or not communicate what they are feeling in a constructive way. In other words, such partners would rather assign a meaning to certain actions than hold an intimate discussion. Remember, intention and actual behavior do not always align, so before questioning the actions, find out the truth that drives them.

Childhood Traits and Relationships

When you are born, you are like a sponge, absorbing habits and patterns of behavior from your parents and environment. Let's say you were born with parents who would often express their love through presents. You may now have shaped an idea that someone who truly loves you should express that through gifts.

Imagine a partner you met has the opposite view on love. Presents for them mean an unnecessary expense. Without clear communication, there may be lots of misinterpretations and conflicts in this connection. Consequently, before you assume what love means to your partner, ask them first.

A negative trait that a child can learn is criticism. Let's say your parents criticized one another much more often than gave praise. That type of behavior, despite its distorted way to express love, may now be imprinted on your subconscious as a way to treat those you love. A relationship imbued with constant criticism may not survive for long and certainly will not bring fulfillment and joy.

That is why it is imperative to learn to shift this negative behavior by interrupting that pattern. If you find yourself in a similar situation, in the moment of trigger, implement a new positive way of responding. Specifically, the next time you have an urge to criticize anyone, sing a song, take multiple deep breaths, call a friend, read a passage from a book, or simply smile. Afterward, when the need for criticism is gone, express yourself in a constructive manner.

This way, you will eventually develop a new pattern and, with enough practice, create a new more powerful method of expression. Also, the more that you work on loving yourself and eradicating limiting beliefs, the faster the need to criticize others will cease. Remember, hurt people hurt others, while healthy and loving people bring love and bliss to others.

Intimacy and Relationships

The strongest and most powerful relationships are built on intimacy. Intimacy is a revelation of the inner self and your ability to open your heart. It can be challenging to be your most authentic self if your heart still harbors wounds and scars from painful past occurrences such as unhealthy relationships or adverse childhood experiences.

Many relationships fail because, during the early stages, partners reveal only their best qualities, sometimes even acting them out. Once these stages pass, some unpleasant personality traits begin revealing themselves, and drama and conflict inevitably arise.

Therefore, the key to building a lasting relationship and friendship is having the courage to expose your weaknesses alongside your strengths, the willingness to work through personal limitations, and the eagerness to embrace that transformation with your partner.

Triggers and Relationships

If you believe that you truly love your partner and you are not in a relationship of codependency or lack of love toward yourself, observe what behavior triggers the conflicts. A truly soulful connection is possible when you learn to release the old, limited self.

Triggers are past wounds. In the moment of inner anguish and intense conflict, you are probably not even talking to your partner, but rather reliving your childhood hardships. As children, we were so dependent on our parents and if we did not feel loved and secure, we may have developed an automatic negative response to certain behavior.

For this reason, discuss with your partner what brings pain to the surface. It may help both of you become more conscious of deep inner wounds, which will help you stop taking things personally in the midst of conflict.

Expectations in Relationships

In order to create a blissful relationship, realize that your past experiences are not your future circumstances. They do, nevertheless, often build your expectations. In other words, when intense negative occurrences take place, some individuals begin unconsciously expecting similar results.

I would like to give you an example. My client Elena had experienced a deep love in the past, yet the relationship didn't last because her partner was simultaneously dating another woman. She was completely heartbroken and spent years grieving until she was finally able to move on. When I met her, Elena was in a fresh, new relationship, yet the shadow of doubt, which was the residue of the last relationship, threatened her new love. That same fear resulted in her pushing the new boyfriend away without any genuine reason for it.

This story teaches you to realize that your past experiences are your lessons or, often, the outcome of a limiting belief rather than your destiny or future conditions. And expecting similar events only strengthens the dark prophecy.

To further understand Elena`s story, it is important to note that when she was eleven, her father left the family for a different woman. So, the seeds of that expectation were actually planted in her childhood and were the initial catalyst for the dysfunctional relationship. Elena unconsciously accepted those experiences as a norm in a romantic relationship because that was all she had known, and then she fostered that dynamic within her own life.

I suggested that Elena look within in order to heal the past, both from her childhood and the previous relationship, and to start working on self-love and confidence. When she sincerely began to believe that she was lovable and magnificent, and once Elena released the past distorted view of a romantic relationship, her previous expectations ceased.

Ultimately, what I would like to add is, when children experience divorce, rejection, the death of a parent, or similar events, they create a limiting belief about their self-worth, which later in life may manifest toxic relationships and patterns of rejection. Remember, though, that your partner is merely your teacher. If they awaken enormous pain or past expectations, that is how much you need to heal. Relationships in a healthy human being should awaken more unconditional love than negativity. If it happens otherwise, limitations are still embedded in your core.

Hormones and Relationships

There are many male and female hormones, but today I would like to talk about testosterone and estrogen, which both play a key role in a healthy relationship. Testosterone is a male hormone that is essential not only for a healthy sexual life but also for a man's general well-being.

A low level of testosterone leads to different physical and mental challenges including depression, lack of sexual vitality, and low motivation. A decreased level of estrogen in women can lead to a variety of health challenges such as premature aging, osteoporosis, heart disease, and most importantly, its influence on a woman's emotional well-being.

In addition to aging, unhealthy lifestyle choices, and lack of physical activity, when a man is not happy with his financial situation and not stable in life, his level of testosterone decreases significantly. If he does not perform enough competitive activities and his significant other is unhappy, his level of testosterone also goes down. For a masculine man, the harmony between him and his romantic partner, as well as their well-being, is highly important for a healthy testosterone level.

My advice for a woman in a committed relationship is to educate her man about what brings contentment and happiness to her soul, as well as to encourage him along the way, and provide constant opportunities to express his masculine qualities such as protectiveness and leadership. It is natural for a woman to test her man, which often comes off as a criticism.

It is essential for a woman to rise above negative reinforcements and learn better ways to communicate. These new changes will positively affect a healthy testosterone level in her partner, which in turn will encourage a vibrant sexual life, a higher level of productivity and financial stability, optimal health, and emotional wellness.

A woman's estrogen level depends on her cycles. These levels drop significantly after ovulation and decrease by the end of menstruation. It is essential for her man to be gentle when she is chemically depleted. It will greatly help her to restore balance and prevent her from entering into an emotional rollercoaster. That is because this is the most sensitive and vulnerable phase in which she needs her partner to be the most nurturing and affectionate.

My advice for men is to be gentle and understanding of a woman's emotional fluctuation as it may be the result of hormonal changes and learn to nurture and express unconditional love and support. This way, the level of estrogen can become more balanced, as well as her emotions.

Realize that feminine nature is naturally unpredictable, and when you give room for all of those feelings to live without being suppressed and judged, you will have the happiest, most loving, and fulfilled woman on earth. In return, you will receive so much joy, sexual pleasure, and genuine encouragement that your relationship will feel miraculous.

Now you can see what an important role testosterone and estrogen hormones play in your partner's mood, sex drive, and overall well-being, and how applying these new skills can greatly improve the quality of your relationship.

Feeling Enough First

Another important truth to realize is that your partner is not there to complete you, as you are already whole and complete. The subconscious belief "I am not enough" often causes individuals to attract partners for the purpose of making them feel more "enough," yet it never works.

If you do not feel complete at your core, you will seek constant validation and approval from others, which often results in drama and conflicts when your needs are not being met. What does it mean to be whole and complete? It is the state in which one feels content and fulfilled. That is also when you love and fully accept yourself. Only at this point will you be able to love someone unconditionally.

Realize that the secret behind any successful relationship is your ability to love and accept someone just as they are rather than constantly attempting to fix them. No one is a perfect person, so instead of getting triggered by certain imperfections, perceive them as a great motivating factor to drive you toward self-improvement every day. Again, your partner`s behavior is often a reflection of your inner state.

I would like to give you an example. A client of mine named Greg is a very successful man by societal standards. He had everything in his life except love, which he had been looking to attract for many years. Greg had met many amazing and wonderful women, yet it never seemed to work.

The reason that he had such a hard time manifesting love was due to his inner state of incompleteness. That same inner feeling of not being or having enough mirrored and attracted the partners who were never enough for him. Recognize that an individual who frequently judges and finds faults in themselves often finds imperfections in others.

Additionally, Greg`s decisions were dictated primarily by his mind rather than his heart. He was always choosing a partner according to status, his mother`s opinions, past experiences, and his beliefs. In other words, Greg closed his heart, which is truly the path to unconditional love and acceptance toward yourself and others, and was no longer able to feel the pure essence of the other person.

How can you possibly expect to fully connect with another when you label and judge them, often based upon your own incompleteness? That is why it is so hard for some individuals to attract and sustain love. There are billions of people in this world, yet if you judge and allow the mind to take over, you will find faults and problems in every encounter.

While some potential partners do indeed have faults that need to be reflected on, that type of a "wrong" partner is frequently a manifestation of your own frequencies, which are shaped by previously formed limitations.

Tame Your Mind

Let's observe how a busy and untamed mind may create conflicts in any relationship. I would like to share a story of Emma. She was in a fresh, new relationship with Richard. One day he was late getting home from work. Emma began inventing crazy stories in her mind in order to explain his absence. Even though Richard texted a reasonable explanation, she just could not let herself believe it was true.

In her nightmare imagination, Richard was probably flirting with some new secretary or old fling. All night Emma was envisioning separation and felt an enormous pain from this illusionary expectation. When Richard got home, she was burning with anger and eventually exploded. All of this happened because Emma had allowed her mind to take control while assuming the worst-case scenario.

What if, instead of assuming, she spent the night in a state of stillness? What if Emma had allowed herself to feel joyful and undisturbed, passionately worked on her favorite project, or simply rested? The outcome could have been completely different.

Each individual is unique, but everyone probably can relate to those negative mind-created stories leading to unnecessary despair. To achieve a beautiful state of serenity and bliss, learn to surrender and realize who you are at the core of your being.

You are not the stories of your mind, you are not your circumstances, and you are not what you do. You are an infinite soul living a human experience. The reason you may be unaware of this is that you probably allow the mind to define your essence.

A hyperactive mind is not yet considered a disease in modern society; rather, it is seen as a normal way of living. In reality, the mind, which is constantly filled with thoughts, especially negative ones, is one of the biggest causes of relationship challenges and separation. Acknowledge that unconditional love cannot reside amid the sea of judgments and assumptions.

Higher Awareness Exercise

I would like to give you an effective exercise to shift into present-moment awareness. Take deep breaths from your heart. Feel the vibration of love filling your heart and rays of love and light radiating through you. Continue breathing love until that is all you feel and until thoughts lose their power and significance.

When you begin living your life in this sacred space, which is a place of unconditional love for yourself and all life's creations, you will be able to manifest and sustain a happy, loving, and fulfilling relationship.

Masculine and Feminine Polarities

Another important aspect to understand in order to create a fulfilling relationship is that frequently the reason partners are strongly attracted to each other is rooted in their differences. According to physics, plus attracts minus. The same is true of any relationship. It is not a coincidence that masculine qualities are so different from feminine ones.

Unfortunately, the same differences that make you attracted to your partner can also cause conflicts. In relationships, women often complain that they are misunderstood and not loved in a proper way, while men often feel underappreciated. It happens because masculine and feminine speak different languages, metaphorically speaking.

Feminine energy is a complex power with varieties of different colors and shapes, while masculine energy is more straightforward. Feminine energy is like an ocean that is changing frequently and may be quite unpredictable. So many factors may hold influence over her emotional well-being such as the lunar phases, monthly cycles, hormones, life's circumstances, astrological impacts, and much more.

For instance, when a woman experiences a highly emotional state and doesn't receive unconditional acceptance from her lover, she may lack the courage to reveal her genuine needs and, instead, become more emotional and even aggressive toward her partner.

Men, without understanding the complexity of feminine nature, may become afraid of their intense emotions and take them personally. And instead of giving the needed unconditional love in order to resolve the conflict, they may instead make matters worse by being combative or completely dismissive. At this point, a man may have on his hands an emotionally hurt woman.

It is instinctual for a feminine nature to test her partner, as she wants to feel protected and secure. And what seems to her man to be harsh criticism may actually be the test of his strength and power.

Can you see how learning about masculine and feminine polarities can improve your relationship? For those who would like to deepen their knowledge on this subject, I would recommend a very powerful book, *The Way of the Superior Man* by David Deida. It is written for men, yet I believe it is beneficial for anyone who wishes to understand the subject more deeply.

Freedom in Relationships

Another essential component to creating a blissful relationship is to allow your partner to experience freedom. Some individuals, when moving into a serious stage of commitment, expect their significant other to give them their full time and attention. This quality doesn`t help you become closer, but quite the opposite: it may actually cause disharmony or other challenges.

Once, I attended a very powerful workshop on relationships that was taught by Michael and Barbara Grossman. They were teaching it while dancing the waltz. Barbara and Michael believe that a healthy relationship is just like a dance; on the right side, the partners are holding each other tight, while on the left side, giving each other enough space.

In a relationship, just like in the waltz, you should build strong intimacy, friendship, and closeness while simultaneously allowing your partner to experience complete and total freedom. For example, you can enjoy some separate hobbies and activities, and even attend certain events on your own. You can also have different circles of friends. And most assuredly, you should give your partner freedom to choose to be themselves and make their own decisions.

There are also times when your partner may prefer a time of solitude in order to gather thoughts, meditate, or alleviate emotional distress. Being together doesn`t always mean you should be doing everything together. On the contrary, doing things separately sometimes gives time for your partner to miss you and to realize what an important role you play in their life.

Possessiveness is a quality that kills any relationship. Understand that your partner is not something that you own but rather a human being who has chosen to be there with you to share delightful memories and to help you grow and evolve. Realize that the more you control your partner, the further away from you they would like to get. In contrast, the more freedom you emanate, the closer with you they wish to be.

Possessiveness and jealousy are rarely about the partner's behavior; rather, they are caused by personal blocks or limiting beliefs, which provoke fears of rejection. Those qualities often result from a lack of self-love and self-confidence. Again, when you feel enough, you no longer feel scared of being rejected or betrayed.

If you believe you have a tendency to be jealous and possessive, please go within and strengthen love for yourself, rather than spending your precious time controlling your partner's behavior.

SEXUAL INTIMACY AND RELATIONSHIPS

Sexual intimacy is essential for a healthy and long-lasting relationship. I believe that the reason many individuals think that passion dies over time is that many couples don't explore and learn this area profoundly. In my opinion, sexual intimacy should grow simultaneously with the expansion of your consciousness.

It is never about merely physical attraction; it is about two spiritually awakened souls exploring a new level of possibilities. And the more you are willing to connect with and learn about your partner, the more layers of depth you can achieve during sexual intimacy.

To explore this powerful area, go beyond merely achieving a physical connection by embracing sacred practices of Tantra, which can lead not only to closeness on a new and completely different level but also to a profound spiritual awakening. In the chapter "Sexuality Is Sacred, Not Sinful," I introduced practical tools on how to master the art of sacred sexuality.

Empathy in Relationships

Another important quality to build an enriching relationship is your ability to feel your partner's needs. Notice when your significant other is tired, angry, or simply not feeling well. Listen to their concerns and give them your undivided attention.

The journey of life can be challenging sometimes, and your partner may need extra support at certain moments. Remember, that is why you are on this beautiful path together—to support, nurture, and cheer each other up. Learn to become empathetic to your partner's needs. Again, the purpose of any relationship is to become stronger together, grow, transform, and progress into more evolved individuals.

When something unpleasant comes to the surface, remind yourself that the current circumstance is mirroring a block or a limiting belief that still needs to be healed and see it as a blessing rather than an obstacle.

In conclusion, a healthy intimate relationship is one of the greatest sources of bliss and fulfillment. Yet it can only be maintained and fostered to its full potential when both individuals are willing to evolve and grow together.

It can be daunting to be in a relationship as you can never be in full control of your partner's behavior. That is why, in order to create a fulfilling connection, you must master your own limitations and invest time and energy into consistent inner growth. Create love toward yourself. Learn to tame your own mind and eradicate limiting beliefs. Master communication skills and gain knowledge of the differences between masculine and feminine polarities.

A relationship is a journey, not a destination, and it is entirely in your hands what sort of path you would like to walk together. Understand that when you are at peace with yourself and the world, when you are confident and successful, when you are motivated and fulfilled, you attract a partner on a similar frequency.

Yet if you are suffering with low self-esteem, a mentality of lack, fears of rejection, and other negative qualities, you often get pulled to the person who will provide what you are radiating and need to heal. To sum it all up, YOU yourself must become the right person to attract what you are seeking.

PART V
DEVELOP LEADERSHIP QUALITIES

CHAPTER 13

MASTER COMMUNICATION SKILLS (PART 1)

> "The art of communication is
> the language of leadership."
> —James Humes

To become successful in everything you do, it is highly beneficial to master communication skills. Many conflicts and misunderstandings occur because of the lack of this essential knowledge. Communication competencies are vital to creating successful relationships in every sphere of life. Luckily, these skills are learnable and, with proper practice, will become a part of your personality.

BECOME A GREAT LISTENER

Many people assume that excellent communicators are those who speak beautifully, with the right articulation and tone of voice.

Those attributes are definitely valuable skills to acquire, yet these are not the most essential qualities that define excellent communicators. Being a great listener is an essential trait to become a successful conversationalist.

The truth is that the majority of people in the world are great when sharing their own experiences rather than listening to others. Some individuals get lost in personal inner monologues, judgments, or assumptions during a conversation. Great communicators, alternatively, are the ones who not only listen but are also sincerely interested in others` stories, opinions, or points of view.

Often "poor listeners" are not even aware of this limiting quality and while the other person is speaking, they are already thinking about the next thing to share. Consequently, the next time you are engaging in a conversation with someone, begin observing how well you listen to the other person.

Listening and not really hearing what the other is expressing is a trait many individuals exhibit, and which shows a lack of attentiveness. Choose instead to intentionally hear what the other person is saying and observe the emotions behind the words.

Discern the Emotions

For many years, I was fortunate enough to be a student of the Meisner acting school, where I learned a very powerful technique: the skill of not only listening to the words being spoken but also the emotions attached to them.

The same expression "I am feeling good" can be said in the emotions of anger, sadness, happiness, or frustration. When you learn to read the feelings behind the words, you are one step closer to building powerful connections.

A personal experience that illustrates this is when I lived in a building where everyone complained about the manager.

According to the other tenants, she was mean and unfriendly, and it was absolutely impossible to befriend her.

In addition to detecting the emotions behind the words, another powerful technique I learned in acting school was the power of non-judgment. Everyone has their own unique story underlying their personal behavior and patterns. Your judgments, nevertheless, can become a barrier to many opportunities as they come from your own view of the situation rather than from a deep empathy and compassion.

One day, for example, I had an opportunity to engage in a short conversation with the supposed "ill-tempered" manager. I asked her, "How was your day?" to which she replied, "Very good." Although her answer was positive, I noticed the emotions of sadness and even anger behind those words.

What usually happens in this type of conversation is that people immediately assume that this type of reply is personal. I discerned that it was coming from her own dissatisfaction and had nothing to do with me. So instead of becoming reactive to the reply, I looked at her sincerely and expressed gratitude for all the wonderful work she did in the building. I noticed immediate warmth in her eyes, and that influenced us to engage in more frequent conversations.

I cannot express enough appreciation for the amazing things the manager did for me. Once, I was leaving town for a few months, and she allowed me to sublet my place to someone, which was contrary to the rental agreement. She would also not charge me for my pets that I adopted at that time. And there were countless other acts of kindness and grace for which I am forever grateful.

I was sincere in my approach toward her and did not seek to manipulate or take advantage. I was authentically interested in my manager's story. She sensed it and opened her heart to me.

Paying attention to the emotions behind words makes people feel noticed and acknowledged because it shows that you sincerely care for them. All authentic connections truly begin with genuinely caring for others rather than pretending that you do.

The Power of Empathy

All human beings, at their core, are capable of feeling compassion and caring for others. Remember the last time you watched a movie that brought out deep emotions inside you. It happened because it is part of human nature to be empathetic. You also have a capacity to "feel" people you encounter in the same way, by learning to listen and care for them with an open heart.

Realize that developing empathetic and compassionate qualities toward others is the doorway to building successful and powerful relationships, which often open the way to infinite opportunities in your life. Helen Keller once said, "Alone, we can do so little; together we can do so much."

In some situations, you could say that people who are rude and impolite toward you do not deserve care and compassion. I remind you again that hurt people hurt others. In other words, it is their inner pain that causes them to behave in less loving ways.

This doesn't mean, though, you have to allow others to treat you unfairly. Instead, you can learn to understand the causes of certain behaviors, help them shift into love, and stop taking things personally.

Body Language

In addition to noticing the emotions behind words, you can learn to observe changes in a speaker's body language as these often occur when they are triggered or reaching a point of particular importance to them. Knowing what the person values and what charges them emotionally are keys to gaining a deeper understanding of the individual.

Becoming aware of body language during a conversation is also the fastest way to build rapport. Rapport is an essential first ingredient to any important discussion as trust is the foundation upon which solid connections are built, and people tend to trust and relate more easily to those who remind them of themselves.

A good way to build rapport quickly is not only to repeat back key words and phrases that you hear someone say but also to subtly reflect their body mannerisms, as well as the speed and tone at which they speak.

It doesn't mean, though, that you should be acting while doing so. Just discover the tone of the other speaker that you can tune in to so that, like two waves on the ocean, you are going in a similar direction and at a similar speed.

If you deal with an emotionally upset person, however, you should not reflect their tone, but stay calm, non-reactive, and relaxed in order to help them shift emotions.

THE DOORS OF OPPORTUNITIES

Recently, one of my friends, Kevin, shared an inspiring story with me. Not long ago, he graduated from university and was hired by a very successful law firm as a legal secretary. Kevin is well-spoken, highly educated, and most importantly, a great communicator. Additionally, he was very dedicated to his job. And even though he was hired as a secretary with a small salary, Kevin pursued this opportunity with passion and enthusiasm.

One day, he received negative and harsh remarks from his boss, Barry, due to a small spelling mistake made in a very important letter. Barry was highly disappointed and expressed discontent in the form of anger.

Kevin is a highly empathetic and attentive person. He observed the body language and the emotions behind Barry's words and noticed that his disappointment was far greater than a small mistake in the letter. He had known his boss for a few months already and was immediately aware that this was not his typical way of expression.

After allowing Barry to finish, without raising his voice and being offended, Kevin apologized for the mistake in the letter and promised to be extra careful in the future. Kevin also expressed admiration for his boss's talents and skills and declared that the disappointment he'd caused brought him great discomfort.

Kevin's response led to the softening of Barry's heart and tone. Afterward, Barry relented and confessed that the spelling mistake was not such a big deal and admitted that the exasperated response had occurred due to a bad day. He even apologized for his harsh tone.

Imagine the same situation with a different reaction from Kevin. What if, instead of being calm and non-defensive, he had gotten overprotective and confrontational? That probably would have led to an argument, conflict, or even a breakdown in their relationship.

Instead, Kevin's effective communication skills led to a strong and powerful friendship with Barry, and soon he even became a highly successful lawyer in the firm. You can see in this story a great example of how excellent communication skills can open infinite possibilities in your life. It also illustrates that genuinely caring for others can create advantageous connections.

GET SINCERELY INTERESTED

To be authentically interested in another person, begin by asking questions about their life. Listen intently, express genuine attentiveness to the story and learn not to interrupt. Interrupting someone is a reflection of not really listening, because when you do so, you have made a conclusion or an assumption, rather than allowing the other to finish their idea. Always remember to be authentic and sincere to avoid creating an impression of having a false motive.

I knew a man who was very lonely, and I wanted to find out the reason why so many people avoided him. I had an opportunity to meet him for lunch and discovered the cause. The entire duration of our time together, he was talking about himself, and when I had a chance to say something, he would interrupt and start speaking about himself again.

Talking about yourself most of the time, especially when others do not ask you, is one of the fastest ways to repel them. If, on the other hand, someone is interested in your story, it is okay to answer their questions and share your experiences. You just have to be aware of the balance of speaking and listening in any conversation, so that both parties feel involved.

CAREER OPPORTUNITY

Here is another example. A client of mine, Anastasia, went to an important meeting. She had a job interview with a company she had dreamed of working for a long time. When Anastasia arrived, she was introduced to the manager, George. At first, she remained silent while paying full attention to the questions he asked.

After each question, Anastasia took a short pause to make sure George had finished his thought process. Speaking immediately after the other person is finished can be interpreted as a form of interruption. Just make sure that the pause feels natural, rather than awkward.

While answering questions, Anastasia expressed genuine intention in working in the company. At the appropriate moment, she expressed appreciation for the opportunity to be interviewed by George.

Anastasia had done extensive research prior to the meeting, and she mentioned how deeply honored she was to be considered by a company with such a great history. George was impressed by Anastasia's demeanor and by her extensive knowledge of the company. In a few days, she was invited to work for them.

I can't deny that in order to get hired for any job, you must know the subject very well and have an appropriate education. Nonetheless, what sets you apart from other competitors is the excellence of your communication skills.

We live in a world with billions of people. What makes some individuals more successful than others? In this new digital age, you may no longer be required to provide certificates and diplomas to get a well-established job. One of the qualities that leads to insurmountable success is outstanding communication skills.

CONFIDENCE AND COMMUNICATION SKILLS

Confidence, which in this context is the outcome of preparation, assists you in becoming an excellent communicator. Let's say you have a job interview for a position as an accountant. Write down all possible questions you could be asked and prepare to answer them in the most skillful ways.

It often happens that, even though you may feel you know all about your sphere of work, when you are in a stressful situation, you may answer the interview questions with less confidence if you are unprepared. In this context, preparation is one of the keys to becoming an excellent communicator.

For a few years, I was an actress and went through many auditions where I was asked personal questions by casting directors. Even though it is almost impossible to forget personal information, I would sometimes stumble and take long pauses.

The reason for this is that when an individual feels under pressure and is surrounded by many interviewers, they may get nervous and stop responding with confidence. That is why when I considered all the possible questions that I may be asked and practiced them until I felt comfortable, I mastered any audition.

Consequently, to prepare for a job interview, write down all possible questions you may be asked and rehearse sufficiently. Only upon completion of this practice will you be ready.

A Book Is Judged by Its Cover

Additionally, be meticulous when going to a job interview or any meeting, especially with someone for the first time. Some individuals spend hours preparing for the opportunity but completely dismiss the importance of their choice of attire.

There is a famous Russian saying: "First impressions are most lasting; a good dress is a card of invitation; a good mind is a letter of recommendation." Understand that if you are well prepared for the interview, yet your clothes are not appropriate according to the sphere of your work, you may create a negative impression. Ultimately, your personal style is an extension of your communication skills.

In conclusion, to become an impactful conversationalist, you should become a great, empathetic listener first and learn to read the emotions behind the words. Studying body language will assist you greatly on this path.

When you are sincerely interested in others' stories and points of view, and are willing to proceed using a nonjudgmental and nonconfrontational approach, infinite doors of opportunity will start opening.

Your confidence level will improve if you spend time preparing for a job interview. Lastly, you will be able to create a beautiful first impression when you continuously polish not only your communication skills but also your style.

CHAPTER 14

MASTER COMMUNICATION SKILLS (PART 2)

> "Communication to a relationship is like oxygen is to life. Without it, it dies."
> — Tony A. Gaskins, Jr.

Learning communication skills is a key to creating lasting and fulfilling relationships. Conflict, drama, and disagreements frequently occur due to a lack of effective communication between partners.

Why do misunderstandings occur in the first place? As previously stated, the reason for this is that each person has unique patterns of thought and behavior which often result in incorrect assumptions.

One of the couples I recently worked with shared their story. Natalie and Daniel were at a conference where they worked together. When the event was almost over, Natalie was summoned to a business gathering that she didn't really want to attend. At the same time, Daniel was invited to have dinner with friends and colleagues. He was unaware that Natalie had decided to skip the meeting and assumed that she was attending it; that is why he did not invite her.

The dinner lasted longer than anticipated, and when Daniel texted Natalie the time of his return, a deep disappointment, and even anger, arose in her heart. She felt hurt not only for not being invited but also for not being asked about her plans for the evening. This reaction completely shocked Daniel due to his lack of awareness of the whole situation.

What happened in this case was simply a miscommunication that led to a night of disappointment and conflict between them. Everything would have turned out differently if Natalie had simply expressed her decision to skip the meeting. With proper communication, Daniel would have been delighted to invite her to the dinner.

This challenge came about because Natalie assumed that Daniel should have asked her whether she had actually committed to attending the meeting. Natalie expected this type of response because that is how she would conduct herself in a similar situation.

It frequently happens that an individual expects the other to behave through their own filters of understanding. Yet, each one of us is brought up in a different culture and upbringing, so what may seem like the right action for one may be perceived as completely inappropriate and ignorant to another.

The realization that your partner does not always think in the same pattern as you is an effective way to avoid conflict-triggering situations. And once you awaken the courage to share your feelings in a polite and authentic way, you will move one step closer to becoming an excellent communicator.

A WIN-WIN RESOLUTION

There is a famous German saying, "You can be right, or you can be rich." For example, in a conflicting situation, it is often more productive to avoid a confrontational reaction and focus on the solution or the outcome you desire, and not the finer points of how you will arrive there.

Looking at the negative aspect of the situation seldom brings resolution. This is not a game, after all, and getting to the desired outcome should not be viewed as a contest or a battle, but rather as a way of finding a solution that makes both parties feel like they've won.

Also, the best manner to point out ways other people can improve is to be polite and constructive. This should result in a win-win for all concerned. When you put someone on the defensive, it becomes much more likely that your point will not get across.

Prior to engaging in a serious conversation, start by highlighting the positive aspects of the other person. The truth is not everyone likes to be told where they need to change. Nevertheless, when you start that type of conversation with a compliment or description of their best qualities, the criticism loses its harshness. This technique works incredibly well.

Let's say a colleague of yours often talks loudly on the phone and it is very disturbing, especially when you need to concentrate. You have asked her several times to speak more quietly, yet her behavior is unchanged. Since the quality of your work is being affected, you decide to have a serious conversation with this coworker.

Before this type of discussion, take a few minutes to consider their best qualities. For example, your colleague may be very honest and generous. Begin the conversation sincerely mentioning how much you admire those qualities, and only then politely explain to them how talking loudly on the phone negatively affects the quality of your work, and *you will be heard.*

Speaking from Your Heart

When you start living life from the sacred space of your heart, it is so much easier to create powerful connections as you start accepting others without judgments and assumptions. In the chapter "Sacred Space of Your Heart," I introduced you to practical and effective skills on how to experience life through the prism of love and appreciation.

When you reside in this state, you stop getting triggered when something doesn't go your way. You stop questioning yourself and others as you start living from a state of elevated awareness.

To learn to speak from your heart, shortly before the conversation begins, imagine breathing back and forth through your heart. Now visualize that it is not air, but rather the light of love moving through you—and with each breath, extend that light further and further out until it reaches the heart of the person you are chatting with. This is what it means to speak from the heart.

If at any moment you find yourself feeling nervous or emotional, return your attention to your breath and your heart and focus on expanding love and appreciation. This way, you will transform any conversation and add great connectivity and depth. Almost any confrontation can be resolved in this manner—not only faster but also in a much more constructive and satisfying way for both parties.

What I have also noticed is that when you do speak from your heart, you rarely say something you should not have as it leads to greater authenticity and a closer connection to the person you are communicating with. Also, speaking from your heart encourages you to shift into a present-moment awareness, which has numerous benefits for your health and well-being.

Let's say you are confronted by someone in a very negative, angry, or demanding tone. It is obviously very unpleasant to find yourself in a situation like this. Unfortunately, many people would take those emotions personally and react in a protective or counteractive manner which frequently escalates the negative emotional state.

If you are centered in your heart, on the other hand, and feel the emotions of love, you will be able to separate the other person's behavior from their true essence, and when you look at the other with the eyes of love, their anger or pain will subside. That is why speaking from your heart is essential in order to eliminate conflicts and drama from your life and instead create authentic and meaningful connections.

A Loving Heart in a Business World

You can obviously imagine how involving the heart and its energy can be useful in almost any sphere of life. There have been many studies on the subject of effective sales. For example, when presentations are driven not by the desire for profit but rather from the point of a genuine aspiration to bring value to a client, the sales figures naturally increase. That is because when you radiate love in your heart, when you authentically care, you build close bonds and form repeated sales or future collaborations.

What about group situations? Public speaking, for example? Just imagine the type of impact you can have on the world when you sincerely care for the transformation of others rather than your performance alone.

What I noticed in my own experience is that every time I share a motivational speech and am governed by the love in my heart rather than my mind, I always create a difference in the auditorium. It happens because I shift the attention from myself to the needs of the listeners.

For that reason, if you find yourself in a situation like this, connect with the whole group through your heart. Truly, we are all one consciousness. Not only will your presentation flow more smoothly and be better received, but you will also experience a new level of depth of universal oneness.

The same is true of any business. Let`s say you are the CEO of a big corporation. If you sincerely care for those who work for you and radiate love, compassion, and gratitude toward them, your team will perform miracles for you on a daily basis.

When an individual is noticed, appreciated, and cared about, they will go the extra mile to perform at the workplace. At this point, they will care for your business just as much as you do, since they have become like family rather than simply an employee.

Love is the strongest force in this universe, not anger, comparison of ourself to another, or any other negative feelings. That is why awakening this powerful emotion in your heart can help you to become not only an outstanding conversationalist but also a more prosperous, happy, and fulfilled individual.

ELEMENTS OF EMOTIONS

Something else to pay attention to is the element of the emotion that is being directed at you. Let`s compare your emotions with elements of nature. In a negative context, anger is fire, stubbornness is earth, lack of interest is water, lack of concentration is air. In a life-affirming context, fire is passion, earth is attentiveness, water is flexibility, and air is positivity.

So, if someone is coming at you with a lot of anger, one of the worst things you can do is lose your cool and use the element of fire. When two people channeling fire meet, all you get is a much bigger flame. The element of water in this situation can be effective in putting out fire calmly and steadfastly as flexibility can modify anger. Also, by implementing positivity, the element of air, you can effortlessly transform any negative situation.

If you are dealing with someone who is very stubborn in their view, rather than pushing harder, you should apply a more flexible approach toward a situation as well, essentially the element of water. That is because your willingness to adapt to that point of view is able to soften a stubborn person. Afterward, you can share your belief gently and effortlessly.

If it feels like the other person is not paying attention to what you are saying, adding some enthusiasm and passion, or the fire element, is the key to engaging them. If you notice that the other person has a hard time concentrating on the information you are providing, it is important to become more attentive to their way of conveying information, which is the element of earth.

In general, I have noticed that becoming more flexible, which is the element of water, is the key to easy and effortless communications and a successful and fulfilled life. I would like to introduce you to my favorite quote from the famous mystic Osho:

"Ask the sands of the oceans from where they have come. They have come from the mountains. They will tell you a great secret: 'Water wins finally. We were hard, and we thought that water cannot win. We were very, very settled; we could not believe that this poor water, so soft, unharming, unhurting, nonviolent could destroy us. But it destroyed us.' That is the beauty of feminine energy. Don't be like a rock. Be like water, soft, feminine. And victory is yours."

To put this in a different context, the more flexible you are in your ability to shift your perspective and adapt to the other person's view, the more powerful a communicator you become.

Right Brain, Left Brain

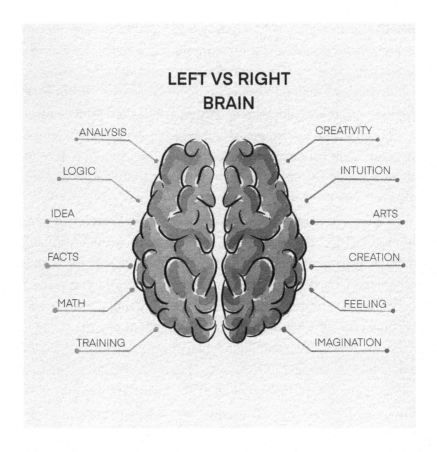

Some individuals tend to be right-brained, while others are more left-brained. Right brainers tend to be more emotional, creative, expressive, and intuitive. Those individuals tend to be highly passionate in conversations, quick to make decisions, and they have an incredible imagination.

Left brainers tend to be more logical, analytical, and objective. Those individuals in conversations usually pay close attention to details, and before any commitment, they do investigative research. Knowing what type of person you are involved in a conversation with will spark a new level of connection.

Additionally, learning which side of the brain influences you is beneficial for making the right choices. Let's say you are a right brainer and are in the process of investing in a new service or a product. You get so excited that you don't take time to think and get enough evidence about the quality of it. Now, you may have made a poor investment. If you are a left brainer, you may do too much research and, as a result, lose the golden opportunity altogether.

In communication with others, if you are a right brainer, you are governed by passion, and it can be hard for you to comprehend an individual who comes across as more analytical. You may even assume that your subject is not interesting to them. That is why understanding of the influence of the brain on the way you communicate will open a new way of acknowledging why others respond differently to the same information.

Another important thing to know while in a conversation with these two different types is that in order to increase interest for a right brainer, you need to apply more passionate and vivid stories. Speaking in this way will excite their brilliant imagination. While speaking with a left brainer, contrarily, providing the essential facts and proofs is the key to a successful outcome.

Ultimately it is about finding balance between the right and left brain. Right brainers should take more time to research and sleep on the final decision, while left brainers should connect more deeply with their heart and intuition so that they don't get stuck primarily in a logical approach.

COMMUNICATION LANGUAGES

While speaking the same language, different individuals may have various communication styles, which are influenced by different cultures, background, environment, and other factors.

For example, in some traditions, greeting each other with a hug is a way to be polite and genuine, while in others, it may be perceived as disrespecting personal space. Knowing you are meeting an individual from a different background, do some research on that culture and the appropriate way to communicate.

Since this information is not always available, I also recommend observing closely how the person you are interacting with communicates and behaves before acting, and you will make a much more powerful first impression.

Individuals from some countries, for example, may express themselves in a louder tone. It is easy to assume that they speak in an aggressive way, but they are simply being themselves.

When I arrived in the U.S. from Russia, I encountered some misunderstandings from American people about the way I communicated. I was perceived by them as too direct and even aggressive. Since then, I have learned that my behavior was misinterpreted. I grew up in a culture where it was quite normal to say the truth boldly, while in American culture, my way of communication was perceived as being rude.

For that reason, before jumping into any assumption about the other person's behavior, become curious about their values, traditions, and ways of expressing themselves. By doing this, it will be just so much easier to become a great conversationalist.

CHOOSE POWER, NOT FORCE

Power will always win out over force for force, requires constant effort and creates resistance, while power simply is. Learn to stop forcing others to do and act according to your expectations. You may encounter too much resistance otherwise. Instead, learn to awaken love in your heart, accept others as they are, and stop constantly attempting to change them.

Understand that when you use power, you accept no for an answer with ease and grace as you can't always make everyone agree with you or provide you with what you are seeking. By using this approach, you are so much more likely to achieve the desired objective, with less effort and much more joy.

When you allow those you encounter to make their own choices without pushing them, they feel acknowledged, respected, and safe with you. And don't be surprised when these individuals will go that extra mile to help you in a time of need. It is because allowing others to have their own individuality creates more profound relationships.

Additionally, learn to acquire knowledge of different viewpoints as this is a fantastic opportunity to broaden your perspective and comprehend fresh approaches to handling and interpreting life's events. I love what Richard Branson, a British entrepreneur, has to say on this subject: "Someone who thinks differently can help to see problems as opportunities and inspire creative energy within a group."

There is another famous quote on the benefits of the power approach from internationally renowned spiritual teacher David R. Hawkins: "Force is limited, whereas power is unlimited. Force is divisive and weakens, whereas power unifies. Power attracts, whereas force repels. Power serves others, whereas force is self-serving."

Therefore, do not deprive yourself of infinite opportunities and profound connections by forcing others. Rather, awaken the power within to accept each individual unconditionally and learn to spread love and compassion.

In conclusion, realize that communication skills are one of the most vital skills you can learn, not only to create success in every area of life but also to awaken peace and harmony in your heart.

To become an excellent conversationalist, learn to speak from your heart while radiating love, compassion, and appreciation. Explore the elements of emotions and learn about the difference between the left and right brain.

Use power rather than force in your approaches and acquire knowledge about various communication styles. Use these skills to empower others through your words and actions and not as a way of manipulation.

I believe that, going forward, you will be much more aware in your communications—both as you listen and as you speak. Practice makes perfect, so be prepared to devote some conscious effort to this ongoing process.

CHAPTER 15

YOUR WORDS HAVE POWER

"When you realize the power of your spoken words, you actualize more powerful experiences."

Spoken words are the seeds that ultimately take root and bloom into the tree that is your destiny. How aware are you of the messages you express in conversations with others? Remember, you first create your reality on an energetic level, and your words and thoughts influence what you build from that invisible realm.

Unfortunately, many people are not conscious of the negative influence they themselves create in their lives by using weak and meaningless words. The fortunate news is that once you are aware of this pattern, it can easily be transformed into a new, more powerful expression.

The Influence of the Words

The words you use most often in your conversations, positively or negatively, affect the manifestation of your dreams. Let's say you often use phrases such as "I can't," "I will try," or "I'm incapable." By doing so, you have already decided you are lacking the ability to perform that specific task. How do you know the truthfulness of those limiting statements without even testing the possibility?

Realize that those declarations shut off your brain's capacity to receive attainable solutions or guidance. When you say, "I can" on the other hand, you open the pathway of infinite possibilities. Meanwhile, simple phrases such as "I am able to," "I am capable of," or "It is within my power to," influence your subconscious mind to work for you, even while you sleep.

When you say, "I will try," what you really are saying is, "I will put some effort in, yet I may not accomplish what I plan to do." When you say, "I will do it," you immediately unlock the capacity for accomplishing the desired outcome.

For that reason, every time you catch yourself using negative phrases, stop and become aware of the fact that they do not serve you but instead create challenges on your path to success. Learn to implement more powerful phrases and words until you create a new positive way of expressing yourself.

Your Words and Your Choices

Did you know that the way you speak about yourself influences your choices and decisions? Let me give you an example. Ashley had a very challenging childhood. Her mother was an alcoholic, and her father was completely absent. Ashley began living an unhealthy lifestyle by indulging in excessive drinking and not being able to hold down a job. In conversations with others, she would often justify her behavior by mentioning childhood trauma, her mother's alcoholism, and her father's lack of support.

Can you see how Ashley gave power to the past to define her current personality traits? What if instead in her conversations with others she said that her mother was an example of what not to become, and as a result, her inspiration? What if instead of being a victim of past circumstances, she rose about those limitations? That change of perspective would positively influence not only her but probably her mother as well.

Realize that your words have enormous power over your behavior. When you speak positively about yourself and your life circumstances, you create a new constructive way of being. I remember I had a very difficult breakup, yet in conversations with others, I awakened the courage to express benefits instead of complaints.

Very soon, I forgot about that experience. I do believe the unpleasant memories and emotional pain dissipated swiftly because my spoken words imprinted an image of a new degree of self-love and respect for myself.

Quit Worrying about Others

Have you ever found yourself worrying about others? Do you know that when you worry about someone, you doubt their ability to create more positive outcomes? Let's say you have a close friend who is going through a challenging time. You may think, "Oh, my poor friend. I wish they were able to survive this heartbreaking experience." Most individuals are governed by pure intention while speaking similar expressions. Nevertheless, the worries we feel for others create a higher possibility of them manifesting.

Some parents do it so often that they unconsciously create negative circumstances for their children. I overheard a few times phrases like these: "Oh, my daughter is killing herself over those exams" and "I am concerned my son will hurt himself skiing on that mountain." Realize that those expressions create a probability of those things taking root in reality. And the more concerned you are, the more you give birth to these likelihoods.

I would like to give you an example. I have worked with an amazing woman named Kristina. She loved her husband more than anything. At the time I met this lovely lady, her spouse was going through a serious illness, and every day she would cry and say, "I will lose my husband."

I informed her that if she continued expressing this fear, she could actually influence the outcome to transpire. Unfortunately, by the time we met, Kristina was already in the habit of believing that she was losing her spouse so strongly that his condition worsened.

I would not deny the husband`s responsibility in regard to the situation, yet I do believe that those who worry for their closest people, especially dwelling in deep emotions, influence their outcomes as well. Let`s become aware of the power of our spoken words to manifest much more favorable experiences.

Your Words Influence Your Outcomes

Realize that the words you use may influence your future. You yourself sometimes speak the undesirable concerns into existence. Oh, I have heard such expressions: "I will not survive those turbulent times," "This job is killing me," or "I will die of happiness."

Now that you are aware of the power of your spoken words, let`s see what the expression "This is killing me" can enact in your life. Your mind doesn`t have a sense of humor and takes everything literally. It creates pathways in the brain, which may ultimately manifest activities that can actually endanger you. It doesn't mean your life will turn into shambles overnight, yet the more you use that limiting expression, the more damage it may create in your life.

I knew a man who used very many negative words and expressions such as, "My children drain my energy," "The bills are killing me," and "I am old." What do you think this man's reality looked like? Exactly the way he was describing it. His children manifested consistent challenges, he struggled with different health conditions, and he looked and felt way older than his age.

What You Allow in Your Energy Field

Have you ever noticed that what a musical artist often sings about is manifested in their life? It is because they unconsciously shape their reality with the words they use. Have you ever thought about whether the music you listen to affects you in any way? When I became aware of what I was allowing in my energy field, my life took a different, more uplifting turn.

There is a very famous rapper in Russia, Timati, whose lyrics often express his high level of confidence. Timati's public persona is that of a very self-assured man. While listening to certain songs of his, my level of self-esteem is boosted, and I feel empowered about my abilities to unleash the highest potential. That is the power of conscious choice.

When I was an actress, I would often receive dark and deeply dramatic roles. Fortunately, I met a very powerful teacher who informed me that those choices were influencing my life negatively. Once I realized this fundamental knowledge, I made a conscious choice to only play positive roles that promoted a new level of being and awakened divine light within me. Interestingly enough, when I started playing princesses, I began receiving more compliments, signifying I had attained a royal frequency.

That is because what you fill your energetic field with, you radiate into the world. Please become aware of the information you allow into your environment. Why create unnecessary roadblocks if you can seemingly choose more positive and uplifting material to influence your consciousness?

Words in Your House

What words adorn your house? Once I was visiting my friend Alex, and I noticed a painting with the expression, "What a mad world." I explained to my dear friend the negative influences that affirmation could produce in his life. He valued my advice and, a few months later, expressed appreciation for this observation. What Alex noticed was that less madness manifested in his reality as soon as the painting was removed.

I highly recommend putting beautiful affirmations all over your house in the form of exquisite paintings, pictures, or cards. You will immediately notice the positive change they create.

For example, in my office, I have cards with words printed on them such as "focus, motivation, and abundance." In the bedroom, I have ones that say "passion, friendship, and love." In my bathroom, I am surrounded by images that express "meditation, serenity, and rest." And in the kitchen, I have cards signifying "blessings, gratitude, and joy."

Become aware of how the attributes of your home affect your life. Those images and affirmations are creating pathways in your subconscious mind without you even realizing it. And it is up to you what patterns you would like to form or strengthen.

CONSCIOUS STYLE

Have you ever considered if the words printed on the clothes you wear may influence you and your environment? Let`s say you wear a shirt with a negative message such as "Angry Dog."

This phrase will now be noticed by those around you, and it radiates far lower frequencies than a positive message. Therefore, make more conscious choices while selecting your style to create a more powerful impact in the world.

SPOKEN WORDS AND THE WORLD

The world is in dire need of positive people who share more empowering messages. Negativity still resides, and in some places even prevails, on our planet because there are many individuals who are conditioned to experience life in a state of stress and agony.

When you went to school, you probably studied geography, mathematics, and other required subjects. Did you study to perceive the world through a positive prism? Probably not, because there is not yet any mandatory subject in school which introduces this valuable skill. Now is the time to become aware of the effect a pessimistic mindset has on your life and on those around you.

Every time you speak negatively, you strengthen limiting patterns, which will soon reflect the reality you talk about. Furthermore, when in conversations with others, spreading negativity is influencing them to build pessimistic views on the situation as well.

Let me give you an example. A woman named Lucy doesn't love New York and, in her conversations, would often mention how many rude people she encountered there and how dangerous the city was. What type of ideas about New York do you suppose Lucy might instill in other people's minds?

Understand that sharing a similar viewpoint multiplies the likelihood of the vison reappearing for the individual who expresses it as well as the possibility of manifesting it for others. In contrast, spreading positivity opens up the potential for beneficial outcomes in both your life and that of others. I believe that the more people awaken to this truth, the more harmonious the world will become, with less havoc and suffering.

Words and Negative Habits

Negative habits are probably familiar to everyone since all of us have experienced them at some point in our life. Have you ever asked yourself how you created and affirmed those patterns? You do so unconsciously, first by witnessing them; afterward, you strengthen those habits with your thoughts, words, and actions. Since this chapter concentrates on the power of words, let's acquire the knowledge of how to use your spoken words to eliminate self-destructive patterns.

This process is illustrated through the following example of Gabriella. She was in the habit of eating sugary cakes every night. If you ever asked her to describe those sweets, she would create the most beautiful picture of them with her words.

What if Gabriella learns to change the associations of what those desserts truly mean to her? What if instead she trains herself to describe that habit as something detrimental to her health and beauty? What if Gabriella creates a new story of her amazing life without any desire for body-wrecking desserts and speaks that vision into existence.

This way, she would soon create a new picture of them in her mind, which would in turn create a decrease in their consumption. The deeper the new picture is embedded, the less the desire will be there. And that is exactly how your spoken words can eliminate negative habits from your life.

Miraculous World

Life and Earth itself is abundant as well as scarce. How often do you talk about this perspective amidst your daily conversations, and what exactly do you decide to express? Marianne Faithfull, an English singer and actress, said it simply and powerfully: "I know for a fact that heaven and hell are here on Earth." This is true of abundance and scarcity.

So many of your experiences are determined by your perception of the world. It is all dependent on what you choose to concentrate on and where you put your attention. Have you heard the expression, "Where focus goes, your energy flows"? Focus on abundance or any other positive aspects for those qualities to envelop your life and the world around you.

Become aware of the daily miracles you experience in every living moment; share this perspective with those around you and awaken them to a higher state of awareness. This way, you will lift your energetic vibrations, while simultaneously elevating the collective consciousness as well.

Speak Your Wishes into Existence

What is your wish? Speak it into existence. Words have enormous power as they channel information from the physical world into the invisible realm. That is why affirmations have been popular for decades.

The modern concept of affirmations has its origins in antiquated religious and cultural customs. A concept that cuts across time and space is the ability of spoken words to bring about positive change. Affirmations are also supported by scientific research, which shows that they can alter the brain`s neural pathways and enhance one`s well-being.

How can you use affirmations to design a new reality? Let`s say you wish to manifest an ideal job. Ask your inner guidance to show you the path to the ideal vocation. Now take a moment and discover the feelings and sensations that a new job awakens.

Relive those emotions as often as possible while simultaneously speaking that wish into existence. You can use powerful phrases such as "An ideal job opportunity opened up for me," or "I am feeling blessed and beyond grateful for manifesting my dream job."

You can use this technique in every situation. What if you are in an area where it is complicated to find parking. Do you immediately assume that there is no parking space available? Or do you believe in the magic of the universe?

From now on, start believing in the best possible outcomes and speak them out into existence. In this example, you can say,

"Parking spots are always so easy to find," "I always find the best parking spot," or "An ideal parking spot is shown to me." By trusting in the ability to realize your wish wholeheartedly, more possibilities to find parking will open up to you.

Any desire or goal you would like to actualize, speak it aloud with passion and enthusiasm, believe you have already manifested it, and be open to receiving those aspirations.

Negative Expectations

Do you expect good or bad things to happen to you? When you speak positively, you have faith in the universe. That is when you verbalize phrases such as "I am guided in miraculous ways," "Everything great comes easy," or "I am always supported."

If you often expect negative outcomes, your words and expressions come in the form of pessimism. Realize that the more you anticipate unpleasant experiences, the more frequently you actualize them. You send out your intentions to the universe in the form of thoughts, feelings, and words.

While using negative expressions, you are unconsciously requesting those outcomes. Oftentimes after manifesting them, you may feel that the universe is unfair to you, yet you were often the one who influenced those circumstances. The good news is, once you are aware of the power of your spoken words, you begin realizing much more favorable outcomes.

In conclusion, spoken words can have a profound impact on your reality and the world around you. The words you speak about yourself can affect your outcomes. The way you describe your experiences can positively or negatively impact your choices and actions.

By becoming conscious of the kind of words you allow into your energetic field through music, art, media, and style, you are able to influence your state and well-being. Also, you can speak your wishes into existence. So, from now on, become aware of your expressions and shape new constructive experiences.

PART VI
STRENGTHEN YOUR INTUITION

CHAPTER 16

SENSING BEYOND THE SENSES

"When you learn to see and hear beyond the unseen, the doors to an effortless path begin to open."

This chapter is about what is probably one of the most vital qualities you are capable of awakening and developing, which is your sixth sense, or your intuition. Intuition is the guidance from Infinite Intelligence which exists within all of us. As Florence Scovel Shinn once said, "Prayer is telephoning to God, and Intuition is God telephoning to you."

Why is this trait so essential? Because life without the right guidance can quickly turn into a series of wrong choices and unnecessary challenges. On the contrary, what if you can often be at the right place at the right time and be consistently guided to make the choices that serve you? This state can be attained through intuitive connection.

To tune in to this sacred gift, it is essential to understand that the logical, rational mind is often the barrier to receiving intuitive insights. That is why it is essential to learn to disassociate from its direct opinions and assumptions.

Logical Mind

As I have mentioned throughout this book, a decision made with merely your rational mind is most often influenced by your past memories. For example, let's say you had a horrible experience last time you worked for a specific company. If you receive an opportunity from that same organization, even if it is in a different location, the previous memory would probably awaken thoughts of doubts and uncertainty.

The opinions of your logical mind are not often based on facts; rather, they are based on past recollections. This job opportunity can be what you have been dreaming about, and despite the fact the company is the same, the experiences can be completely different. And in this case, listening to your intuition can be a highly beneficial tool as it can lead you to the best decision.

That is why connecting with your intuitive guidance means eliminating unnecessary worries and wrong assumptions. Intuitive knowledge may not make sense to your logical mind, yet it is your guide to the path of least resistance.

Understand that your previous memories are a very small part of your existence. Expecting similar results is a personal choice, which may become a roadblock to exciting possibilities. The logical mind is a useful tool, yet often it is used incorrectly. So instead of analyzing your expectations, connect with a higher level of awareness and ask for rebirth of the intuitive nature you were once born with.

Distinguish Intuitive Messages

Many individuals find it difficult to trust intuitive guidance since those messages are invisible and can be perceived irrationally. And how do you know which messages come to you from your intuition and which from your intellectual mind? Each individual is different and has their own unique way of receiving their intuitive guidance. I will provide you with the most common ways.

Clairaudience—these messages come as a soft and calm voice.

Clairvoyance—these messages arrive as an image or a scene.

Clairsentience—these messages come through as a feeling and an ability to tap into the emotional energy of others.

Claircognizance—these messages come as a feeling of just knowing. To state it differently, you are aware yet not clear how you acquired the knowledge.

Intuition Is Your Natural Gift

Knowing the way you receive intuitive guidance is vital in order to awaken your sixth sense. When you are born, you are naturally highly intuitive. Unfortunately, the insights often get suppressed as you may not always receive proper education on how to harness your sacred gift. Any talent you don't utilize eventually becomes weaker. Anything you practice, in contrast, transforms into a stronger and more effective skill.

The other reason some individuals lose touch with their sixth sense is that it is more common for humans to rely on the logical or rational mind while making important decisions. Let's say you are drawn to study art. Your deep passion for something is usually a form of intuitive guidance.

However, your friends and parents say that your passion is not profitable, and instead they persuade you to study business or medicine. Your intuition guides you into your true essence, yet you listen to the opinions of others or their intellectual minds while your whole essence, your whole being, belongs to the world of creativity.

When you stop trusting your intuitive voice, it lessens. That is when intellect takes over. There is nothing wrong with an intellectual mind, yet its knowledge can be narrow. While using intellect, you logically decide what is best for you. It may feel safe to make a rational choice, yet that choice may not always be what's best for the expansion of your consciousness and ultimate success.

The Influence of Mind

The mind can be very tricky because it is often programmed by your environment, education, and past experiences, which may provide false ideas and beliefs. I mention throughout this book that inherited limiting patterns influence negative responses to challenges and pessimistic perceptions of life.

We are not often taught to live our life in a state of detachment from the mind. To the contrary, it is more common to view reality through the prism of the mind. This way is often a distorted way of seeing reality as it is based on what you already know rather than an expanded perception.

Intuition or your guidance cannot be heard in this state because the mind is too distracted with the loud thoughts and can't define which one is the right message, so it keeps analyzing them. It is like a soup with multiple ingredients that has been boiling for many hours. The cabbage is there, but you cannot really find it among other overcooked vegetables.

Mysterious World of Intuition

That is why it is essential to realize that in order to define the messages from your sixth sense, you have to silence the intellectual mind and tune in to the mysterious world of intuition. How do you do so? It begins with the decision to reawaken your sacred gift.

Realize that intuitive guidance is where your wisdom resides, the wisdom that will take you further than years of studying and searching. The mind has answers for everything, but are those answers correct and beneficial ones? I believe that living solitarily in the mind is the fastest way to the life of self-destruction.

This is what we may observe happening in the world. There are some people who find themselves so lost in the mind that they are *lost in life*. They search and seek answers and satisfaction somewhere outside of themselves, and without realizing it, they are moving further away from whatever they are seeking.

Mindless State

That is why on a path of intuition, you have to begin practicing a mindless state. This is the state where you detach from your thoughts. When busy thoughts occur, let them pass without letting them into your heart. This state is possible to achieve with a consistent awareness.

One of my favorite quotes from Osho has a lot of wisdom on this subject: "Watch from your inner sky and let the clouds float. Become just a watcher. And remember, the clouds will come and go, you can remain indifferent." I love this analogy very much. As you can see, Osho compares your state of awareness with the inner sky and your thoughts with the clouds.

Remember, fighting with the mind or attempting to stop thinking is a form of resentment, which allows the pattern to persist. Watching the mind, on the contrary, is surrendering or choosing a path of serenity in which distinguishing intuitive messages becomes effortless and natural.

Your Intuitive Guidance

As I said earlier, we all receive answers differently. To discover your way, notice how you receive your guidance. Begin this journey by tuning into a state of higher consciousness, or a mindless state. Afterward, begin by asking questions. Start with small, less important ones throughout the day.

For example, before going to work in the morning you may ask, "What color shirt is the receptionist wearing today?" Pay close attention to how you receive the answers. The right guidance may feel like a high, soft voice, and the wrong answer is a normal or slightly deeper voice. Notice the difference between the wrong and the right answers. Notice how they appear in you. And remember the answer may not come right away. You may receive it while doing some activity right before leaving to go to work, or on your way there.

The ways to receive the answers are unique for each individual, but I believe by paying close attention to the process, you will deepen your connection with your intuitive guidance and learn to distinguish those messages.

Intuition Exercise

Another powerful technique to practice intuition is through an exercise with a friend. Ask them to hold a number in their mind and provide you with the range. For example, your friend may hold in mind number 8, and they should let you know that it is between 2 and 15. Attempt to guess this number.

Do not get frustrated if you do not approximate the right answer immediately. I once attended an intuition class in which we did similar exercises for three days. On the first day, many attendees frequently made mistakes while making predictions. On the second day, fewer and fewer inaccurate responses were made.

On the third day, the questions were more challenging. For example, in one of the inquiries, we were supposed to describe an unknown person's personality traits and characteristics just by a name and picture alone. Nevertheless, only few people were incorrect after practicing this powerful exercise for three days straight. Remember, an intuitive gift is your natural gift, and exercises like these merely assist in awakening what is already within you.

YOUR HIGHEST FREQUENCY

Your intuition is your highest frequency. The two chakras, or the energy centers, which are associated with this guidance are third eye and crown chakras, the first of which is located around the center of the forehead, parallel to the middle of the eyebrows, and the other on the top of your head.

I do believe that the highest points of these chakra positions are equal to experiencing life at the highest frequencies such as love, abundance, and fulfillment, while the intention behind practicing your intuitive gift should occur from a state of benevolence and integrity.

To say it differently, if your purpose is to manipulate and bring harm to others with the use of this effective skill, you will simply never become great at it. Intuition exists in the space where no lower emotions and destructive thoughts reside because they are, just like two opposite points, located at different levels.

Intuition and Dreams

Another powerful tool to strengthen your intuitive abilities is your dreams. When you are dreaming, you stop thinking, and that is when you are fully connected with the higher realm. Not every dream, however, is teaching or communicating something. Oftentimes a dream can be the outcome of certain unconscious fears or assimilation of new information.

How do you connect to your intuition with the help of your dreams? Before going to sleep, ask a question for which you are seeking clarification. For instance, "Should I hire the person I interviewed today for the position of sales representative? Will they serve the company in the most proficient way?"

Let's say you saw a shark in the dream. Don't decide to interpret the dream directly. In a general context, a shark is a predator, and it can symbolize a manipulative person who may deceive and harm. Nevertheless, before making any conclusions, ask yourself the following question: "What is my personal relationship with sharks?"

Do you see them as dangerous or intelligent animals? Or maybe you associate them with undeniable power. By answering this question, you will discover why you saw them in the dream and how it can relate to the question you asked.

In addition, notice in what form the fish appeared in your dream. For example, if you were feeding the shark and are afraid of them, you are giving too much power to your fears and spending energy in the wrong direction.

Another common dream we all may experience is the death of someone. This is not necessarily a bad dream. Often it actually represents a rebirth. So instead of feeling threatened by it, ask yourself a question: "How do I relate to the person who passed away in my dream? What does this individual represent in my life?"

Let's say your dearest friend died in your dream. This insight can be interpreted in various ways depending upon your feelings, actions, and the environment in the vision. One interpretation could be that you are overly attached to the person or that you are afraid of losing love. The dream may also portend a forthcoming rebirth in your partnership, potentially involving a deeper spiritual bond.

It may additionally mean that your friend is experiencing some health challenges and is sending you unconscious telepathic messages about their fears. On the deepest level, we are all connected, especially with the closest people in our life, so they may be communicating with you through the dream.

Moreover, as you can see, each dream has multiple interpretations. And with enough practice, you will surely be able to define the meaning of them. If you are not clear, ask your intuitive guidance for clarification: "What is the message of this dream?" Afterward, be open to receive the answer through sometimes unexpected ways. As the Persian poet Rumi said, "Everything in the universe is within you. Ask all from yourself."

Another important thing to know when you use dreams to discover intuitive messages is that it's vital to have a piece of paper next to your bed to write down what you dreamed about as soon as you wake up. This is very important because you may forget your dreams otherwise.

A Powerful Insight

I would like to give you a personal example of the power of dreams. Once I was invited to teach a retreat in Bali. The offer was fascinating, yet I had a strange negative inner feeling. I asked a question before going to sleep if it was a good idea to follow through with the opportunity. In the dream, I saw huge, threatening waves in a dark, restless ocean.

It was a clear indication that the retreat may not flow smoothly, and I actually said no. Later I found out from a friend who was the teacher there that the event was not well organized, and she even told me that I had made the right choice by not attending it. Many people didn't show up, some of the speakers were put together in the same room, and the energy in general was quite negative.

If you still have any doubts about utilizing dreams as an intuitive guide, read stories of how some famous people used them to receive guidance on important decisions. For example, there are well-known individuals such as Nikola Tesla, Albert Einstein, Paul McCartney, Robert Louis Stevenson, and many more who used their dreams to receive powerful ideas, which are perceived as supernatural by many individuals.

Nature and Intuition

Another powerful way to become intuitive is by connecting with nature. The best way to do it is by finding time to visit nature reserves. Connecting with the sky, plants, and birds is important to awaken intuition. As Buddha said, "If we could see the miracle of a single flower clearly, our whole life would change."

The miracle of a flower, and all nature in general, is in its pure divine presence. It is not trying to be; it is just being. It is not holding on to anger against anything or anyone; it simply allows life to happen through it.

That is how every element of nature exists. This is why nature is the greatest teacher of present-moment awareness, which can show you how to detach from logical thoughts, and as a result, assist you in connecting more deeply with your intuitive guidance.

Animals Are Naturally Gifted

Did you know that animals are actually very intuitive? It is unknown how exactly they receive their messages, yet it frequently happens that they stay unharmed during natural disasters. Wild creatures often sense what is coming ahead of time and escape if needed. It is my belief that they do not have restless minds, and therefore, do not disconnect themselves from the guidance of the Universal Consciousness.

That is why in a famous tale, "The Magic Swan Geese" collected by Alexander Afanasyev, when a brother was stolen away, his sister, while looking for him, asked nature to guide her. She asked an apple tree, a river, and a mouse to show her the way to save her brother and was able to find him with their support.

I know you may say that I am referring to fairy tales, which are based on fantasy rather than reality. I believe, though, numerous fantasies are the outcome of the author seeing the invisible reality, which has a lot to teach humanity. As nature and animals are the teachers of presence and conscious awareness, they ultimately influence us to awaken and strengthen intuitive awareness.

Intuitive Attributes

Another way to enhance your intuition is with the use of essential oils, herbs, and crystals. I would like to provide you with my list of effective attributes.

Jasmine essential oil is a symbol of the full moon and the night. It is a very powerful oil to use during meditation for increasing your intuitive abilities.

Lavender oil assists in cleansing negative energies and helps to open up the third eye.

Acacia, orange, and *anise oils* help greatly to develop intuitive abilities.

Mugwort is a powerful herb for raising low vibrational frequencies that may stand in the way of clear intuitive insights.

Lemongrass is an excellent herb for opening up portals to intuitive guidance.

Rose quartz is an excellent stone for learning to open your heart and receive intuitive messages.

Lapis lazuli assists with opening the third eye.

Amethyst strengthens connection with Infinite Intelligence.

There are many other oils, herbs, and crystals that can assist you greatly on your path. If they are beneficial tools for you, trust that you will be guided to discover and obtain the right ones.

Ways to Use Intuitive Attributes

How can you enhance intuitive abilities by using the attributes? You can create a pleasant aroma by adding essential oils in a diffuser during meditation, bath rituals, or other spiritual activities. You can sprinkle a pillow with essential oils or add some herbs under it before going to sleep. You can also add a few drops of essential oils to your skin. Make sure you test products by first putting a small amount on your wrist to see if you have any irritation or an allergic reaction.

You can hold crystals on any part of your body or simply place them next to you during meditation or any sacred practice. You can also wear jewelry with specific stones that can strengthen your intuitive abilities. Additionally, while burning a candle, you can set an intention and put a few drops of oil, little crystals, or a small number of herbs on it.

The herbs can also be used in tea, which can assist you with tuning into a deeply meditative state. You can also make a very powerful bath with herbs, crystals, and essential oils. My favorite is a mugwort, amethyst, and lavender oil bath, which not only detoxes the body but also cleanses you energetically.

Rest and Receive

Rest is a vital way to receive intuitive messages. When you learn to rest and surrender, you become a channel of divine guidance. So many people, especially ambitious ones, dismiss this vital area.

During the early stages of writing this book, I recall having a strict work ethic and not letting myself take breaks. At that moment I realized that I was not allowing the flow of ideas to pass through me. Instead, I was pushing them away.

When I started making consistent time to relax and surrender, great ideas started flowing through me, ideas that I had not even imagined receiving. It felt like in the moment of rest I tuned in to a genius mind and everything I felt puzzled about was suddenly revealed to me.

That is the power of rest and surrender. That is the power of trusting in divine timing, which helped me to write this book and enabled me to bring about many other powerful creations. Remind yourself that balance is the key to a successful, blissful, and fulfilled life.

In conclusion, to attune to your sacred gift, intuition, you should practice transmuting yourself to a higher level of consciousness, which exists in every one of us and, therefore, is possible to achieve.

The more you learn how to detach from your mind, the easier it will be to distinguish intuitive messages. The more you open your heart and start trusting the potential of the invisible forces, the faster your gift will be reborn. Nature, your dreams, intuitive exercises, and attributes will assist you greatly on this journey. Lastly, rest and surrender will help you to become the channeler of intuitive messages.

CHAPTER 17

JUST ASK!

"Often the solution lies in rightly asked questions."

Life is a game that turns out to be a magnificent adventure for those who not only learn but embrace its rules. You may ask, "How can I begin living that type of reality?" We live in the age of information, and yes, powerful knowledge is available to all of us. There are schools, private mentors, online courses, and books that can guide you on this journey.

How do you know, nevertheless, what knowledge will help you move faster toward freedom from limitations? Do you know which choice will open the doorway to happiness, confidence, spiritual evolution, abundance, or whatever else you are seeking?

Different Paths

It is believed that there is a universal system of success such as diligent work and an unshakable belief in oneself. And as I already mentioned in this book, this system works for some individuals but is insufficient for others. Why? It is because we all have different paths and lessons, which we inevitably experience on our journey.

Let's look at the path toward success of some famous actors. For example, Sylvester Stallone's acting career started with him writing a screenplay for the movie *Rocky* in which he intended to play the main character.

He was offered more than $300,000 for the script, yet despite being completely broke, refused to sell it unless he could play Rocky, the main character. After several attempts, Stallone's demands were heard, but his salary went from $300,000 to $35,000. He was willing to sacrifice the large salary for the opportunity to play the main character, which led to the launch of his successful A-list career.

Harrison Ford was unsatisfied with his acting career due to consistent hardships on his journey. He became a professional carpenter to support his family. The universe, though, had a different vision for him. While installing a wooden door at Francis Ford Coppola's house, Ford was hired for the role of Han Solo in *Star Wars*, which started a very successful acting career.

Chris Pratt worked at a Bubba Gump Shrimp Company restaurant. One day, actress Rae Dawn Chong turned up at the restaurant. Chris approached her and, after introducing himself as an actor, asked if she had any opportunities for him. Just imagine, Chong was in the process of directing a movie in LA and invited Chris to the casting of *Cursed Part 3*, which launched his A-list Hollywood career.

Furthermore, if you ask more people about their stories, you will clearly see how each has their own unique journey. This phenomenon happens in every sphere of life. In the case of finding love, for instance, the advice often given is to visit dating websites or start going out to places where you can socialize with new people. This may be beneficial for some individuals but a complete waste of time for others.

ALCHEMIST OF YOUR DESTINY

The question then arises, "How can you find your unique path to become an alchemist of your destiny?" How do you discover the most effortless and enjoyable path toward the realization of your dreams?

As I stated previously, intuition is the answer. I am aware that believing in something that is intangible is not always easy. This is the reason you should delve deeply into the enigmatic origins of creation in order to awaken this connection.

Let's brainstorm on this subject by asking a philosophical question: "How did you appear in this physical reality?" The answer is simple: from your parents. If you reflect more deeply, though, other questions may arise, such as "What is the purpose of human existence?," "How and why did the first human ever appear in this reality?"

The reason that looking into this subject is so important is that answering these questions from an expanded consciousness will assist you in the realization of the invisible forces that coexist with us as the essential part of this reality. This insight, in turn, will help you break the barrier that stands in the way of you and your intuitive guidance.

Also, when you realize that the purpose of human existence goes way beyond just making money or becoming "successful," unconditional love, present-moment awareness, and fulfillment take place. When you understand that you came here to be a part of a community that, when united and working together in love, will create a profound positive change in the world, you are one step closer to the realization of your dreams.

Is Suffering Necessary?

I would like to bring your attention to another very powerful question: "What is the purpose of suffering?" So many individuals choose the path of unnecessary pain instead of the highest level of awareness, or the path of least resistance. According to Buddha, the root of all suffering is attachment. A very powerful statement indeed, since when you stop being attached, nothing can truly hurt you.

Nonetheless, we are all on a different level of spiritual evolution. When an individual is still struggling with deeply rooted limited beliefs, it is more challenging to achieve detachment as those beliefs typically result in a distorted perception of reality. The fly, for instance, enjoys decaying materials but is not attracted to the smell, taste, and beauty of the rose because it has been hard-wired to be attracted to decaying materials, and decaying materials are all it has ever known.

That is why in order to discover the effortless path, you should expand your consciousness beyond the seen reality. Have you ever contemplated a perspective in which the intelligence that created you also knows the secret code to your freedom and happiness, and that is where the answers should be sought out?

That same intelligence is not something outside of you since everything in the universe is interconnected. It is, in fact, your ability to experience life from a state of higher awareness in which you are able to receive and recognize the guidance from Higher Power.

From a different perspective, it is also possible that you yourself create a holographic illusion called life. In this theory, you believe in the hologram so much that you stop perceiving it as an illusion. It becomes your reality.

And since you may find yourself disconnected from the Source of all Creation, or God, or Infinite Intelligence, or Higher Power, or whatever you may call it, you forget that you are yourself projecting that reality. As a result, you may create (likely unknowingly) turbulence, imbalances, and suffering.

How do we awaken the inner power? How do we attain peace and harmony within our souls? How do we find our way out of spiritual poverty and suffering? Let`s learn to connect with intuitive guidance and discover these answers.

Ask—Receive

How do you connect with your inner guidance? The answer is simple—just ask. Asking questions is one of the most effective ways to discover what you are looking for. Just please always remember to ask from an expanded consciousness.

A few individuals may feel skeptical about this. If you still doubt the invisible forces that coexist to guide and support you, it is okay not to practice asking questions. The reason for this is that your belief is as powerful as the unseen forces. If you don`t believe in something, it simply may not be manifested or provided to you.

On the contrary, if you are ready to increase your intuitive insights, manifest your heart`s desires, and achieve freedom from any limitations, you should begin learning and practicing this essential skill.

Really, what is there to lose? And if it works, you`ll gain more effortless problem-solving skills, begin making wiser decisions, and awaken natural manifesting abilities. And, surely, you will have a better knowledge of something new and exhilarating for you. Your internal potential is waiting to be unlocked!

The Art of Asking Questions

You may be wondering, "What type of questions should I be asking and how should I ask them correctly?" Throughout the day, you are constantly making decisions: some ordinary, some life-changing. Some individuals discover that when presented with options, they may feel stuck, which occasionally causes them to make the incorrect choice.

What are the questions you are facing currently? Let's begin with simple yes-or-no questions. For example: Dear Higher Power, Creation, (or whatever you believe you are communicating with), should I go to an event I am invited to on Friday? Should I consider this particular move? Is the job I am about to be interviewed for a great opportunity for me?

How do you receive the answers to these questions? I will show you various effective ways to do so in this chapter. What is essential to remember is that the key to be able to recognize the answers is to live your life in a state of higher consciousness.

Again, this is the state in which you disconnect from constant mind chatter and instead experience life feeling love and appreciation. This is when doubts dissipate while ultimate trust takes over and receiving intuitive answers becomes second nature.

State of Higher Consciousness

To learn this powerful state is a journey. In most cases, it is a consistent practice of meditation, detachment from the mind, achievement of an inner state of love for all creation, and true understanding of the interconnection and unity of everything in the universe.

It is a state of expanded awareness when not knowing becomes the source of knowing. It is a state when judgments and assumptions lose their significance and disappear from your daily habits.

Even though it takes practice and dedication to begin living your life from this powerful state, it does not mean that you should wait to achieve it before starting to ask questions.

Practicing and developing the ability to receive the answers will simultaneously speed up your path to a higher state of consciousness. The beginning of this eminent practice itself can be considered a part of learning to experience life from a state of conscious awareness.

Intuitive Hunch

A very powerful way to receive an answer to the question you asked is through an intuitive hunch, which can be described as a "gut feeling," or your ability to feel something without conscious reasoning.

For example, there was a moment in the past when I felt lost and deeply unhappy about my life`s circumstances. That is when I asked for a solution to stop that challenging period. I had a hunch to join a very high-class gym.

At that time, I had limited financial resources due to being a full-time student. And while the idea sounded appealing, a one-year membership commitment stirred internal doubts and made me ponder. Then I asked another question from my intuitive guidance about whether it would be beneficial for me to join that specific gym.

After a few days, I had an even stronger hunch. Only this time I had a feeling to call the gym to ask more questions about its membership. Accidentally, though, I called the wrong location, which was actually much better because this gym had a saltwater pool. Even though it was a little farther away, the answer was clear for me: I should sign up for membership at this new location.

In this example, you can see how my answer didn't really come as a clear yes or no but as a feeling or an internal hunch. Also, while asking questions, I could feel that some invisible forces began guiding me to the right decision.

How did I accidentally call a different gym? It still remains a mystery, even for me. Nonetheless, a meeting that occurred there created a life-changing transformation which I was seeking and asking for. That is when I also realized that I would never dismiss intuitive hunches since they always serve me as a guide to the most fulfilled path.

Your Body Is Your Guide

The second way to receive an answer is by becoming aware of your energy body, which is a form of non-physical matter consisting of your aura and chakra system.

Let's say you are asking a yes-or-no question. Now look at your hand and choose any finger you prefer. Ask your intuitive guidance to show you the answer, and while asking a question, feel for a reaction. If the answer is yes, you should feel an increase of the energy in the finger, and it should lift slightly. If the answer is no, there will be no increase of energy. Your finger will feel nothing or may even drop slightly.

Please be patient with yourself if you feel nothing at first during this exercise as there are individuals who are highly sensitive to energy just as there are those who hardly feel it. In the next sections, "Etheric Body" and "Feel your Energy," I will introduce you to an effective way to deepen your connection with your energetic body which will greatly assist you in this process.

Etheric Body

The etheric body is another name for the energy body. Ultimately, it is a living aura that is invisible to the naked eye. Once you learn to feel your energy body, you will become not only more intuitive, but you also will be capable of shifting self-destructive and negative frequencies in your aura.

The best way to connect with and notice your energetic field is through daily meditation. This practice means different things for different people. The central point is the one I already introduced to you in the previous chapters: you should learn to detach from your own thoughts by becoming an observer of them rather than the one who experiences them. It is the state of observation or silence rather than deep and intense thinking. That is when you shift into a higher state of awareness and when you can feel your energy.

The more you tune in to this state, the more sensitive to energy you will become. Additionally, you will be able to discern between those individuals who emit positive versus negative vibrations, which will enable you to make far better decisions in all of your relationships.

What does energy feel like? It feels different for everyone. Some may feel a tingling sensation, a flow of light, arrays of colors, or even changes of temperature in some areas. I am certain you can discover your own way to sense energy once you commit to this practice.

Feel Your Energy Exercise

Sit in a comfortable position. Close your eyes and take eight deep breaths. Notice the energy that is surrounding you. How does it feel? Now hold your hands closely together, like you are holding a circle in between them.

Notice if you can detect the circle of energy.

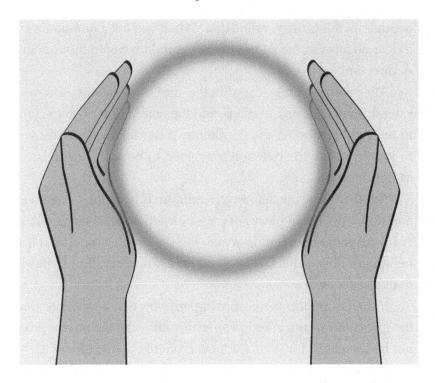

Afterward, spread your hands farther apart. Those of you who are already sensitive to energy should feel the circle of it growing each time you put your hands farther apart.

Questions and Pendulums

Another way of asking questions is by using a pendulum. A pendulum is a weight hung from a fixed point so that it can swing freely backward and forward. I recommend using a violet, dark blue, or clear crystal pendulum since crystals of those colors help you improve intuitive abilities, though you can choose any color you are drawn toward.

To learn to use a pendulum, ask a question with a very clean answer. For example, I could ask a pendulum if my name is Oxana. The answer is obviously yes. Depending on the direction of the pendulum, this is my yes direction. When you ask a question with a clear no answer, the course of the pendulum would indicate the *no* direction.

After you become clear about *yes* and *no* directions, now you can ask any yes or no questions, and the pendulum will guide you to the right answer. If the pendulum is not following either yes or no directions, the question may need to be asked again later, as it is uncertain.

Another way you can use a pendulum is by writing down yes and no on two small pieces of paper placed opposite each other. Ask your intuition to guide you to the right answer and hold the pendulum above them. The pendulum will naturally be drawn to either yes or no.

If the pendulum is not moving anywhere, it is possible that the question was not asked properly or knowing the answer may not be beneficial for your spiritual evolution at this moment.

Can you trust a pendulum fully and completely? If you are experiencing life at your highest vibrations, then the answer is yes. What I mean is, for instance, let's say you asked a question while residing in a busy and desperate state of mind. This way, you are vibrating on a lower frequency, and the answer from the pendulum may not necessarily be the answer from Infinite Intelligence.

Again, the daily work of surrendering and releasing the parts of yourself that stand in the way of a conscious state of awareness is the key to awakening the higher level of intuition and guidance.

Complex Questions

So far you have been practicing asking yes-or-no questions. How do you receive the answers to more complex questions? Let's have a look at this example. Michelle, a beautiful young lady, had a hard time deciding how to set herself free from the financial debts she had accumulated.

I recommended her to ask a question from her intuitive guidance such as, "What is the most effortless and enjoyable way for me to manifest prosperity that will enable me to cover all my debts in the amount of $47,000 dollars while also living joyfully and abundantly?" Notice how we formulated the question. It was specific enough, yet not limited. For example, we could have asked for one particular way to clear debts such as winning the lottery.

Realize that you might not always know what course of action is the best one to take, or what choices you need to make. Your intuitive guidance, on the contrary, always knows and helps you materialize what is best for you.

The question can be written down, said out loud, or simply felt inside. Whatever you choose to do. The most important thing is to be open to receiving the answers without any attachments, judgments, or expectations toward them.

Also, timing is essential as well. It is better not to be overly attached to any specific day yet know and state the period of time in which you would like the guidance or support to be delivered in your life. The answers may come in various ways, and you have to realize that certain requests may need some time to be seen in physical form.

For example, in Michelle`s story, she received a hunch to move across the country. This was something she had been thinking about for quite a long time yet suddenly had the strength to do despite the fact that moving didn`t seem like a good idea in her situation. She needed to apply for another loan to do so. Michelle trusted the guidance and actually did all the necessary steps to relocate. Within a year, she was not only able to pay off the debts but also begin living an abundant life.

Remember, when you ask a question, you do not receive merely the answers but often strength and courage as well. That is why the answer may sometimes come in the form of awakened motivation and ultimate trust in your decision.

With regard to Michelle, this move was a very positive step in her career since it led to another miracle–she discovered her life's purpose. How did it all begin? At first, Michelle rented a room from a very nice old lady, who appeared to have a sick dog. Michelle fell in love with the dog and wanted to find ways to improve his health.

Since traditional medicine had failed, as she was informed by the dog's owner, Michelle began researching holistic medicine. She changed his diet, started incorporating different herbs and elixirs, and the dog began feeling better and better every day.

During this healing process, Michelle realized that she loved caring for and healing animals, so she decided to become a holistic veterinarian. For the first time in many years, she felt such excitement and pure joy. Michelle later told me that there was not enough time in the day for all the passions and projects that suddenly awakened in her. This was another proof that one of the highest sources of fulfillment and joy is following your life's purpose.

Can you see how Michelle's enthusiasm and dedication opened the doors to so many opportunities? Understand that when you ask a question, have ultimate trust, and are willing to take the necessary actions there are invisible doors that higher forces open for you to walk through, whether they be ideas, money, or other fortunate opportunities.

In conclusion, asking questions is a very powerful tool to discover whatever you are seeking. There are various tools and techniques such as pendulum and different energy exercises that you can use to obtain intuitive guidance.

Just Ask!

Just never forget to practice quieting the chaos and storm of everyday life within the mind and learn to experience moments of stillness to discover what you are searching for.

CHAPTER 18

POWERFUL CREATIONS

*"To discover great things, relax and connect
with the still, small voice within."*

Have you ever read breathtaking stories of success that resulted from intuition? So many geniuses, such as Albert Einstein, Nikola Tesla, Henry Ford, and others believed that the reason for their enormous success was acting on their gut feeling. There are also those who may not be aware that they are guided. Nevertheless, it is my belief that it is far more difficult to generate or direct powerful ideas if you are not in touch with your sixth sense.

As I mentioned earlier, Albert Einstein was a great believer in intuition. He would sit in the bath for hours, playing with the soap bubbles to disconnect from his busy mind in order to discover powerful insights. You are probably aware of Einstein's groundbreaking quantum theory of light and his special theory of relativity.

Why would such a great genius spend so much time in the bath? Because he understood the power of relaxation. In this powerful, mindless state, it is so much easier to channel and recognize great ideas.

When you are constantly using your mind to make a decision or discover an answer, you expend too much energy. This way, you may feel more fatigued and allow less creativity to flow through you. Also, while using the logical mind solely, you frequently make assumptions, which may lead to unnecessary challenges or inaccurate conclusions.

The Power of Dreams

Einstein did not only love baths; he also believed in the power of dreams, which can be the portals to intuitive messages. After the dream where he was sledding down a mountain at the speed of light, Einstein discovered the famous Theory of Relativity.

Another famous inventor, Dmitri Mendeleev, struggled to find a pattern using the logical mind. His goal was to organize the chemical elements, and the answer actually came to him in a dream. Mendeleev said, "In a dream I saw a table where all the elements fell into place as required. Awakening, I immediately wrote it down on a piece of paper."

It is scary sometimes to simply trust a dream. I understand because I was once hesitant to base a significant decision solely on a dream. Nonetheless, the more I practiced acknowledging the existence of my intuition and learning to discern it from the voice and the visions of my inner critic, the more reliable this skill became.

Intuitive Geniuses

Steve Jobs, a pioneer of the computer revolution, had a profound piece of advice for humanity: "Don`t let the noise of others` opinions drown out your own inner voice." I agree with Jobs and believe that this world is full of opinions which may lead your inner guidance to subside.

When something happens in life, some individuals immediately turn to trusted people for advice. Counsel can be valuable in many situations, yet I do strongly believe that a more profound answer can always be found within. And by studying many powerful people, this concept was ingrained even deeper into my understanding of the principles of a successful life.

By way of illustration, Jobs was inspired by Indian culture, which combined deep spiritual upbringings and low material values. That is how he learned to connect with his sacred gift, intuition, resulting in Jobs's education taking a different turn.

In my opinion, that was exactly what led him to become a genius of our time. Often, the world of materiality is what disconnects us from intuitive talent as some people lose touch with their inner selves in the process of building their estate.

Oprah is a big believer of intuition as she once said, "I have trusted the still, small voice of intuition my entire life. And the only time I've made mistakes is when I didn't listen." The series of moves and decisions Oprah made by listening to her heart and sixth sense led her on the path of a remarkable journey.

Her other advice to humanity is, "When you don't know what to do, do nothing. Get quiet so you can hear the still, small voice—your inner GPS guiding you to true north."

Your Inner Voice

It is my belief that your intuition is one of the fastest and most effective maps on your journey to fulfillment. While deciding with your logical mind what is best for you, you may not always feel satisfaction after obtaining what you desired.

As I mentioned earlier, when you make a decision based solely on the rational mind, it is most often based on the limited knowledge you have learned from what you had previously experienced. When you ask your intuition about the right path for you, you may be shocked to receive irrational answers about the forward direction. If you follow this guidance, though, you frequently manifest outcomes that exceed even your imagination.

I would like to retell the story of my profound awakening. For many years, I was pursuing an acting career, which was the desire of my logical mind. I later realized that the desire came from a limiting subconscious belief: I didn't feel enough, so I was seeking external validation.

That is when I asked Higher Intelligence to guide me to the right and most fulfilling path for me. And that is exactly when I was led in the most inexplicable way to one of the most spiritual places on earth, Mount Shasta, where I discovered my true life's purpose: transformational coaching.

That is also when numerous miracles began taking place. In contrast, when I was pursuing acting, I would constantly encounter obstacles and difficulties. So, my own experiences strengthened the trust and the belief that, when you are attuned to the powerful wisdom of your intuition, the path becomes so much more effortless and enjoyable.

Intuition and Positive Outcomes

Henry Ford was a huge believer in intuition. When he first had the idea to create a car, he had very little success in the beginning. While listening and feeling connected with his intuition, instead of giving up, Ford doubled his employees' wages.

His inner circle was shocked by this decision and tried to make him change his mind. Yet, Ford felt and saw a different future for the company. That vision eventually manifested a reality in which he became the founder of the hugely successful Ford Motor Company.

Trusting intuitive guidance helped Winston Churchill to save his personnel. While dining at 10 Downing Street in London, a German bomb landed close by. Churchill had a strong impulse to ask his staff to leave the kitchen. In a few minutes, another bomb landed at that particular location. Thankfully, all his employees were saved because Churchill acted on the inner hunch.

Richard Branson, who is one of the richest men in the world, once said, "I rely far more on gut instincts than researching huge amounts of statistics." Richard Branson is founder of the Virgin Group, which has expanded into many diverse sectors from travel to telecommunications, health to banking, and music to leisure.

American filmmaker David Lynch once said, "Intuition is the key to everything: painting, filmmaking, business—everything. I think you could have an intellectual ability, but if you can sharpen your intuition, which they say is emotion and intellect joining together, then a knowingness occurs." Lynch created remarkable masterpieces such as *Mulholland Drive* and *Blue Velvet*.

Steven Spielberg, a highly successful director who created films such as *Jurassic Park* and *Lincoln*, also has confidence in intuition. This is what he said about the sixth sense: "Your intuition is different from your conscience. They work in tandem, but here's the distinction. Your conscience shouts, 'Here's what you should do,' while your intuition whispers, 'Here's what you could do.' Listen to that voice that tells you what you could do." This is such a powerful statement as it refers to possibilities rather than needs. I strongly believe that entering into the world of intuition is akin to stepping into the world of unlimited possibilities.

Jonas Salk finalized the development of the polio vaccine in 1955, and as a result, saved countless people across the world. Despite the fact that medicine relies on science, he relied on the power of intuition. This is what Salk said on this subject: "This is mysterious. I cannot visually, with my physical eye, see the forces that act upon me from within and without, and yet I cannot deny their existence. If I try, I suffer. If I surrender, allowing them to act upon me, and if I work with them, I feel exhilarated; I become filled with the joy of life."

An Easy Path

Just imagine how much time and vital energy you can save on important tasks when you learn to trust your intuition. Just imagine how many wrong choices can be prevented by being intuitively guided. Just imagine how fast the solutions to any problem can be channeled if you don't waste your precious time overthinking. I believe now is a perfect moment to decide to have ultimate trust that the right answers will be revealed to you and reawaken your sacred gift.

In conclusion, you can clearly see how great leaders of both past and present created great masterpieces that continue to excite human imagination. Those are miraculous phenomena that are, at their core, outcomes of intuitive insights.

I honestly believe that every great invention in this world is the result of intuition. Someone had an inner message and had the courage to pursue the idea. For that reason, develop your ability to tune in to the enigmatic realm of intuition, as it holds the secrets to all the solutions.

PART VII
AWAKEN TO YOUR SACRED PURPOSE

CHAPTER 19

THE POWER OF BEING PRESENT

"Being present means becoming one with life and allowing your natural state of serenity and bliss to prevail."

The most powerful state that can ever be achieved is a state of serenity and peace in the now. In other words, learning to be present and detach yourself from your own thoughts. While living in a fast-paced world, it is so easy to forget that being present is your most natural state. That is only when you are able to fully appreciate any accomplishments, acknowledge your surroundings, or simply pause and take a breath.

Since this state is unknown to many individuals, when they encounter a moment when nothing is scheduled, they often find themselves bored or restless and fill this time with various activities to shift the internal unease. This need for activity arises because a busy mind is still perceived as a norm for many people. And the easiest way to dismiss the thoughts is to be occupied with work, shopping, cleaning, planning, or other vigorous activities.

Inner Monologues

Many individuals assume that their inner monologues define who they are and that every thought that comes through their minds contains the truth about them. Unfortunately, not every idea flowing through the mind is positive. Sometimes thoughts are based on fear and negativity.

The number of people suffering from depression, anxiety, or other similar conditions grows year after year. The reason for this is that a constantly thinking mind causes unease and general dissatisfaction. Some individuals experience this state at some moments, while others feel restlessness consistently.

The purpose of life, in my opinion, is to acquire peace in the now, without which the outer manifestations of life will not fulfill your deepest needs. I don`t mean that manifestations of physical needs are not part of a fulfilled life. What I mean is that without feeling complete in one`s heart or feeling present, no matter how much an individual achieves on the outer material level, it will never feel like enough.

That is why in order to achieve a state of presence, it is necessary to separate yourself from your own mind that can never exist in the now. Start observing your thoughts today, and you will see that the majority of them are associated with either the past or future.

Sacred Space of Your Heart

Being present means experiencing life from the sacred space of your heart. Again, it is a powerful state of love and connectedness with all life`s creations. And the best way to achieve this state is by shifting from living in the mind to learning to feel unconditional love, appreciation, and trust in your heart. That is when you become an inattentive observer of your thoughts as those high frequency emotions in your heart have the potential to win out over the mind`s chatter.

AUTHENTIC ABUNDANCE

Since the mind can only see what it is programmed to see, it perceives physical reality through a prism that frequently distorts actuality. For example, some may believe that obtaining material objects and things will make them happy and fulfilled. Remember, the thinking mind is rarely satisfied. After achieving a goal, it is common to feel satisfied and fulfilled for a while before you may begin looking for other ways to appease the voice in your head.

Realize that a prosperous person is not the one who makes millions of dollars, but rather the one who feels abundant. Some rich individuals obtained their wealth through a feeling of not being enough. They perceived material wealth as a way to prove themselves to the world, and many of them later found out that happiness and fulfillment did not follow along. The material world can never help you feel more whole unless a state of attainment is achieved first. And this beautiful state is just so much easier to reach through present-moment awareness.

There is nothing wrong with being prosperous and successful. It is just that if you obtained success, and deep inside you keep searching and looking for things to make you happy and peaceful, you are not truly successful. You didn`t find the serenity and bliss that is within you, and therefore, deep inside, material affluence added nothing to how you feel. In some cases, this type of achievement separated you even further from your true essence. I would call this type of success "surface success."

Surface Success

A great example of attaining *surface success* was my client Annabelle, who came to me in tears for one simple reason: she could not enjoy life and feel happy. For the last fifteen years, Annabelle had worked intensively in order to create financial security for her family.

She raised two daughters on her own, and one of the greatest motivations for her financial prosperity was to provide the best education for them so that they would have the life she never had. Annabelle soon found herself living in the world of wealth, yet deep inside felt even more miserable and helpless.

The reason for her unhappiness was that Annabelle put all her attention toward the world of *surface success*. She never took the time to go within her heart to feel love and appreciation for all her accomplishments or be emotionally present with her daughters.

Instead, she chose to be preoccupied with goals and lost herself in that obsession. Annabelle thought she was expressing love toward her children by providing material affluence, yet that is exactly what made them become more distant and insensitive.

It is like when you buy a new house and put all your effort and attention into making it more beautiful, but only from the outside. Then the house does look like a palace due to the daily work, yet when you go inside, there is mess and dirt everywhere, since you never found the time to take care of it from inside.

A Fulfilled Success

That is why in order to create a fulfilled success, you should find a balance of the inner and the outer worlds. What is essential to know is that the inner has far greater influence on the outer. The inner is like the roots of a tree, without which, it simply won`t exist.

Without an inner feeling of abundance, you will never be truly abundant, even if you own the whole world. As a matter of fact, even if you do achieve massive financial success while having an impoverished internal world, your sense of accomplishment can quickly turn to a constant nagging fear of losing everything you have worked for. Furthermore, the fear can actually be manifested. That is why becoming present is essential not only for fulfilled but also stable success.

Unpredictable Circumstances

Life can be unpredictable. You don't always foresee the next challenge or stressful situation. Even the most enlightened person on earth may encounter turbulence. Nevertheless, an individual who learns to experience life being present becomes an observer of a situation rather than a reactor.

As the mind loses its influence over one's inner state, an individual stops responding with anger or other negative emotions toward unpleasant occurrences. The non-resistant approach makes it simple to transform negative experiences into blessings.

There are two ways of handling a challenging situation. One is by accepting and learning from it, and the other is by resisting and, therefore, recreating it. Accepting means being okay with whatever happened and managing to look at it calmly.

Realize that without the influence of strong negative emotions, you can discover the best possible ways to handle any challenge. In contrast, resisting means being negatively affected by turbulent circumstances and continuing to worsen them by playing them over and over again in the mind.

Remember, the mind's interpretation of the problem inflates the degree of suffering. When you experience life while being fully present, in comparison, the challenges lose their intensity. Without the influence of mind chatter, the natural state of your heart is love. When you experience life through this prism, negative events lose the power to make an emotional impact.

The reason that problems stop having a dramatic impact on your well-being in this powerful state is that you shift into a different dimension of consciousness where you alter your values into what is truly meaningful in life.

In this higher frequency, there is no time except the present-moment. It is when you shift from being attached to the ways things happen to being filled with appreciation and wonder for life itself. That is exactly what lessens the urge for unnecessary suffering. Realize every part of nature resides in this state, undisturbed by life`s challenges, and the more you are able to attune to that way of being, the less turbulence will be created along your journey.

STATE OF AWARENESS

The present-moment state can also be called a state of awareness. This is when you become conscious of the inner voice and realize its often distorted view of reality. Specifically, the stories of the inner voice stop having a negative effect on how you interpret life.

While practicing being present, many people decide to stop thinking completely. It is nearly impossible because that is not how the mind works. Instead, begin practicing the exercise I introduced to you earlier which will assist you in becoming an observer of your thoughts.

Take a breath and hold it in your heart center. Learn to breathe from your heart as often as possible and teach yourself to feel love. When disturbing thoughts come through your mind, shift your focus onto love and appreciation.

Observe those thoughts from this sacred space and you will soon notice how unimportant they are. Again, your repetitive thoughts are merely habits and perceptions based on the past rather than the true facts about you.

Mind's Purpose

You may then ask a question: "What is the purpose of the mind?" The mind has a vital role in your journey and can be used as an extremely powerful tool. For example, setting goals or learning something without the help of it will be an entirely different experience.

Just remember that the same mind that can help you manifest goals, transform limiting beliefs, and perform other important tasks can also make you unhappy, sick, and even insane. Often those who live completely in their minds tend to take every event of their life too seriously and frequently experience dramatic ups and downs.

Elevated Emotions

Strong emotions can influence your destiny. When you feel sadness, bitterness, or anger deeply and extensively, you invite them into your future. As I previously mentioned, your feelings, not your thoughts, have a far greater influence on your outcomes.

Thus, another advantage of present-moment awareness is the lessening effect of negative thoughts on your emotional well-being. What usually provokes intense negative feelings? Something that has happened in the past; for instance, somebody may have betrayed you, and you may feel humiliated and sad. Attachment to the ideal outcome may create fears and pain as something may not go your way. Something may happen in the present such as the loss of a job, or an unexpected negative phone call that creates an emotional outburst. All kinds of situations can create stress and pain. Are those emotions truly necessary?

I once spoke with a very wise man when he was in his 90s. "If I could change anything in my life, I would not waste my time on useless worries," he said to me. Age can be a great teacher as significant wisdom follows it. Why wait though? Instead, decide today to practice being present, which will become your second nature over time.

Remember, everything in life is temporary, and your perception of reality is not really reality itself. The same situation may be seen as the greatest blessing or the biggest sorrow. The one who discovers a blessing or an opportunity to advance in every situation resides in a completely different state of being. Those individuals live their lives with conscious awareness, and, therefore, in the present-moment.

The other way you can describe this way of living is a state of childlike innocence and bliss. You don't always have to understand everything as understanding is often a perception, and conscious awareness arises out of non-judgment.

Innocence and Bliss

The reason children attract so much attention and affection is that they know how to enjoy life to its fullest. Think about a little child who is creating a piece of art or playing a game. The child is always fully present and joyful. They are not trying to prove something to others and are not concerned about the outcome, and for that reason, naturally reside in mindless awareness. The child is completely absorbed in the creation of beautiful art.

The reason that children are so joyful and carefree is that they are purely innocent, and much fewer negative thoughts are yet known to their developing minds. Also, their interpretation of every situation rarely leads to any judgment but to curiosity.

What it truly means is that a peaceful state is not something you should only learn but also remember. That is why, by unlearning the negative habits you may have acquired throughout your lifetime, the state of childlike innocence and curiosity will start shining again.

Remember yourself as a child and how you felt at that time. You were always present in everything you did. You were often joyful, and even if something had happened, such as the loss of a toy, it would not disturb you for a long time.

As a child, you were also like a sponge, learning how to live your life from the environment surrounding you. Most likely, in childhood, you were not introduced to spiritual practices such as meditation and present-moment awareness, so as an adult, it probably became easy to lose yourself in restless activities of the mind.

Steps to Experience the Present-moment

1. How do you achieve a state of undisturbed presence? It starts with the realization of what you have learned in this chapter—an association with every thought in your mind is not a part of your identity, and it is not your inborn state. Rather, it is what you have learned and acquired. This awareness is the first step to freedom.
2. Another powerful step is conscious breath, the importance of which I mention multiple times in this book as it assists in elevating you to a higher state. Take a few very deep breaths right now and shift your attention into your heart by breathing through it. Feel unconditional love and gratitude for the miraculous part of existence which you

are. Disconnect from your thoughts by observing them or simply by overpowering them with a positive inner state.
3. You can experience the present-moment by spending some time in nature and listening to its sounds. I would like to remind you again that everything in nature is present and vigorously alive. By observing it without judgment, you learn to awaken a new state within. Breathing love through your heart and learning to stay in this awareness while being in coherency with nature will awaken a state of vastness inside your heart. In other words, while nothing seems to be happening, such as constant thoughts, worries, or other mind activities, you feel more whole than ever before, and that is when less turns into *more*.
4. The other powerful tool to create present-moment awareness is learning to detach. An attachment to anything creates pain, unease, and tension. You can find yourself overly attached to a perception of yourself, material possessions, or the ideal version of life. That is when your state turns into a disillusioned concept of self and reality. That is when your feelings get easily affected by what is happening in the outer world.

You are not always in control of life's conditions. Recognize, though, that you possess the power to end the mind-created illusions. So, to transform the continual need to control the outer circumstances, shift into your heart and transcend the illusionary suffering.

Realize that by practicing detachment, you will free yourself from negative emotions and experiences. With this awareness, you are not bound to any certain outcomes, and you release yourself from hardships that come as a result of attachment.

When you are attached, you are not present but rather somewhere in a future vision, which you don't have complete trust in. Doubts and fears cloud your reality. *With non-attachment, you become the vision, as ultimate faith prevails.*

Take at least five minutes each day to tune in to this state. It may seem unfamiliar at first, but the more glimpses of a mindless, detached state you experience, the higher your level of awareness will be. Life then becomes an abundance of rich experiences and speechless moments and a new blissful state of being takes over.

THE PRESENT-MOMENT AND GRATITUDE

If you can't see miracles everywhere, just go outside and walk around and notice the comfort that you live in. For the majority of human existence, people had to hunt for their food, live outside without comfortable accommodation, and frequently were not able to survive even the mildest of illnesses due to lack of essential medicine and knowledge.

Have you ever noticed with all your senses the beauty of this abundant planet, and what it provided for you? Warmth, existence, pure water and food, remarkable places, medicine, and truly everything that you need. You live in a world where everything is created for you: supermarkets, drugstores, beauty salons, and so many other things that help you enjoy life.

Yet, it can be easy to take everything for granted and overlook the reasons to feel appreciative. If you cannot feel grateful because you feel that your life's circumstances do not seem to satisfy you, remember, this viewpoint emerges from the perception you choose. Your life's story is the state of awareness you unconsciously mirror.

When you achieve a state of higher consciousness, though, your values change. Achievements and material possessions turn into a game and not the means of defining the state of being. A natural feeling of appreciation for this beautiful existence starts governing your life.

It is understandable that it is harder to create stillness in your mind and feel gratitude when you are in debt, or when you spend your whole day working at a job that you dislike or maintaining an unfulfilling relationship. At those moments, realize that by dwelling on those circumstances, you are living in the past and, thus, recreating similar outcomes in the future.

In contrast, feeling appreciation is feeling present and living a life of bliss and fulfillment. Again, whatever is happening in your current reality may simply be a perception that can be easily changed once the identification with every thought is interrupted.

Remember, life is too extraordinary to experience it from a limited perspective. As philosopher Henry David Thoreau once said, "It is not what you look at that matters, it is what you see." Experience life from a state of still presence, appreciation, and unconditional love to see everything as a miracle and manifest a new miraculous reality as a result.

In conclusion, an awareness of the present-moment is the doorway to not only acquiring your wishes but also experiencing attainment and elation in every moment of existence. In this powerful state, each moment becomes precious as life itself. Present-moment awareness does not require things to be perfect to enjoy the journey to its fullest.

The mind is not designed to live in a state of satisfaction, so shift your attention to a feeling of unconditional love and appreciation to experience life in a sense of bliss and harmony. Practice deep breathing and not-attachment toward anything, even to your own sense of identity. Connect with nature, which is your greatest teacher of serenity and contentment, and realize that you are not your thoughts, rather infinite abundant consciousness.

CHAPTER 20

DISCOVER YOUR LIFE'S PURPOSE

*"You came to this earth to share your
special gifts with the world."*

Have you discovered your life's purpose? If the answer is no, do not be hard on yourself as everyone comes to this realization at a different moment. Occasionally, one may pursue a career to create comfort and stability, and later find themselves greatly dissatisfied, as the only way to genuinely find contentment is to pursue your life's purpose.

One of the biggest causes of depression is not pursuing your calling. In contrast, when you have a purpose in life, you are driven by a reason for being and enthusiasm, and are seldom affected by obstacles in your path. Additionally, that's when Higher Intelligence offers you the greatest assistance.

When pursuing your true purpose, it's important to remember not to get lost in purely materialistic pursuits, but to consistently polish the gifts you are meant to share with the world and to expand your consciousness in all that you do. That's how abundance will follow your actions. Understand that your level of prosperity will increase proportionately to the extent of the service, value, and transformation you provide.

WHY ARE YOU HERE?

Every part of nature has its purpose. The trees release oxygen by absorbing carbon dioxide and, as a result, create cleaner and healthier air. Turtles play an important part in the vitality of the ocean by regulating other organisms. Mosquitos pollinate plants and are the source of food for other species. Spiders control insects and in doing so, protect crops. Microbes ferment foods and produce enzymes and other bioactive compounds. Salmon help to provide rivers with the needed marine nutrients due to their migration habits.

Everything in nature reaches its fullest potential. Trees don't decide to stop growing; they effortlessly do so. Flowers bloom as often as they can. Birds fly as high as they were created to without limits or fears.

Every part of nature is also deeply connected to its purpose without being educated about it. After a mother salmon gives birth to her children, she dies. Afterward, thousands of fish repeat a similar cycle, that of their parents, without being taught.

If every element on earth exists in a divine synchronicity and follows its purpose so effortlessly, then I believe each one of us came here with a higher purpose as well: to serve and support the structure of the world. Once we all awaken to the realization of our own unique roles and the higher purpose behind them, the earth will restore its natural balance, and abundance, harmony, and peace will transpire.

Harmonious Nature

In nature everything lives in total and complete harmony. Flowers don't compare themselves with each other in a state of jealousy and negativity. Lions don't kill other animals for fun but merely as a way to feed themselves and their children. Almost every creature of nature lives in a state of trust in being provided with food, water, and shelter.

I believe that one of the major imbalances nature experiences is caused by humans and is the result of the shift in societal values from oneness to isolation and materiality. Because some individuals are disconnected from this truth, they have lost one of the most powerful ways of living—experiencing life through the state of compassion, unity, and love.

Effortless Being

Your purpose is your divine plan. When it rises from a higher level of awareness, you stop struggling as struggle is often the result of poor intentions. What governs your intention for success? When your purpose is to create transformation, you rise above all limitations. You stop questioning divine timing and being overly attached to the final outcome. That is when you follow your path effortlessly and joyfully.

Imagine you pursue a medical career, and your sole purpose is to receive recognition in that field. Is it truly an authentic goal? There is nothing wrong with looking toward some rewards or accomplishments. I just believe that this particular intention may have appeared from the need to validate yourself rather than from your true calling.

You are here to transform, not to impress, and to transform not only others but also yourself. When you reach that understanding, fears, comparison, jealousy, and other low vibrational emotions have far less power over you. That is when the need to force and prove yourself disappears and your work becomes the biggest source of joy and inspiration instead of desperate attachment to a certain result.

Follow Your Heart

Each individual has their own unique path while discovering life's purpose. Always remember to follow your heart rather than your mind while deciding it. As I mentioned earlier, when you use your mind solely, you apply a logical and rational view to the future, which is not always the best for you.

On the contrary, when you follow your heart, you open up infinite possibilities for a life of bliss and fulfillment and, therefore, ultimate success. Remember, each individual is unique and special and came to this earth to share their gifts with the world. When you are aware of those gifts and use them, you become aligned with the universe and begin to experience a natural flow of manifestation.

Discover Your Purpose

How do you discover your purpose? It begins with the realization that often the barrier to following your higher calling is the overwhelming sense of responsibility in the material world. That is why tuning in to your intuition and expanding your perspective beyond what is seen will assist you to find what you are you looking for.

I would like to provide you with an example. Tom was unclear about his life's purpose. He liked many different activities such as music, writing, and graphic design yet didn't know which one should be considered as the best career choice.

I recommended that he ask his own intuitive guidance and develop an unshakable trust in receiving the answer. Tom followed my advice dutifully and, afterward, incidentally heard from the owner of the restaurant he worked at that they were looking for a graphic designer for an online promotion.

Tom felt a hunch to mention his knowledge of the subject and expressed an interest in pursuing the project. The owner trusted him with the new idea. Subsequently, Tom not only masterfully completed the task but also discovered his purpose. That is the power of intuition.

Receiving the Intuitive Answers

I would like to remind you that there are two ways to receive intuitive insights: one is when you are not attached to the answers, and the other is demanding or impatiently waiting for the answers.

When you are not attached, you become a vessel through which Infinite Intelligence manifests. That is when you develop trust in receiving the answers at the right time, space, and sequence. Conversely, when you are attached, you become desperate and may confuse the answers of your mind with the insights of divine guidance.

What Do You Love Doing?

One way to find your life's purpose is to ask yourself the following question: "If I were financially secure for the rest of my life and would no longer have to go to work, what vocation would I choose?"

If the answer you envision doesn't yet correlate with your current career, don't get frustrated. Instead of dwelling on the negative aspect of this situation, shift your attention to your life's purpose, and ask yourself another question: "What can I do today to become closer to living my true purpose?" Also realize that your current job may be a stepping stone that is preparing you for your calling.

Devotion to Your Purpose

Each day, devote fifteen minutes to one hour or more to your life's purpose. For example, I know a very talented girl, Alice, who was struggling financially. She worked as a waitress in a small restaurant and dreamed of becoming a successful artist.

I recommended that Alice devote time daily to her passion and paint her future with images of love, abundance, and effortless manifestation. Whatever it meant for her. So, every night after work, she started painting her dreams. That is when she was guided to a well-paying job at a very prestigious restaurant, allowing her to take care of her responsibilities and progress with her passion.

This is an example of the invisible support from the universe. When you get passionate about your purpose and begin taking steps toward it, the doorways of infinite opportunities and divine guidance start opening up.

Start Living Your Purpose

When you discover your purpose, don't wait to start living it. If your calling is, let's say, to be a cook, start cooking. Begin practicing those skills even if it's just for your friends. If you desire to be a doctor, begin reading anatomy books or other educational materials to prepare you for school and excite your imagination.

When I started my transformation coaching career, I would mentor anyone who wanted to learn from me, and sometimes I didn't even charge for it. This way, I not only gathered experience and feedback but also eventually created so many referrals that I am now constantly blessed with opportunities to transform and live abundantly.

MASTER YOUR SKILLS

When the purpose is clear, learn to become a master at your given talents. Without practice, your gifts will weaken. Let's say you are a talented dancer. Nevertheless, without consistent practice, knowledge of choreography, and great coordination, it may be hard to move effortlessly.

The practice by itself may feel less exciting. Once, however, you master all the steps, you become completely absorbed in the dance. That is when you uncover new levels of profound fulfillment, joy, and achievement.

EYES OF LOVE

Do you perceive others as competition? Do you feel superior or inferior to other people? Do you compare your success and good luck with theirs? Realize that the more you admire and become inspired by other people's accomplishments, the higher you shift your frequency, which, in turn, opens the possibilities for your own growth and success. Also, what you wish for others, you really attract to yourself.

Another aspect to realize is that the world that is governed by love has a much stronger foundation. When you discover your purpose, a powerful collaboration with others will only lead to expansion and advancement. And what you desire you can achieve much faster because you are so much stronger in unity.

Ask for Help

So many individuals are afraid to ask for help. That is one of the reasons for missed opportunities. There are those who have traveled a similar path you are on, and their guidance may lead to a greater outcome.

Being afraid of rejection is living your life in a state of fear. Remember the concept I introduced to you earlier. Imagine you go to a store with the intention of buying a particular item. Is something wrong with other items? No, you just have a special preference.

When you ask for something and receive a rejection, it may be because they simply are unable to fulfill your request with their knowledge and current resources to assist at this time. When you overcome fear of asking for help, that is when one opened door may become an invitation to the world of expanded potential.

Embrace Your Purpose

Get out of the habit of classifying certain careers. Every calling is a blessing. Whatever you came to this earth to do, that is what you are best at. You can transform the world and yourself through any profession when you pursue it with passion. There is no small work; there are only small attitudes or perceptions.

In conclusion, your life's purpose is why you were born onto this earth. Each individual obtains unique and special talents and gifts, and there is so much you can contribute to the world when you begin using them. When you start living your purpose and commit to it wholeheartedly, you manifest abundance effortlessly.

To discover your calling, familiarize yourself with your intuition, learn to follow your heart, and get inspired by others' accomplishments. Notice the activities that you would perform without the need for financial gratifications, as they can lead you to discover your purpose. Realize that fulfillment, success, and happiness are the result of following your divinely designed path with love, passion, and integrity.

CHAPTER 21

REACHING THE SACRED APEX

"Knowledge isn't power until it is applied."
— Dale Carnegie

You have learned powerful skills and strategies for achieving success and fulfillment in every facet of your life: health and prosperity, sexuality and creativity, confidence and willpower, love and relationships, communication skills, intuitive abilities, and higher consciousness. What's next? Mastery is not arrival at a point where you know all you need to but rather a decision to continue evolving and polishing new skills through dedicated actions.

I have met individuals who, after attending a transformational workshop, decided it had given them all necessary knowledge and, as a result, they stopped improving and exerting effort. Realize that the only way to advance and shape a new more powerful you is through daily commitment.

Obtaining equilibrium in each facet of life is a way to continuous mastery. Working on the seven areas of your life is the key to fulfilled success. It may seem like an overwhelming task at first. Once, however, you start feeling how much easier it becomes to manifest your desires from a new state, you will soon realize that it is just much more effective to put effort into self-improvement rather than in never-ending struggle. Recognize that recurring similar challenges you may experience are often the result of a lack of commitment toward personal development.

Design a Plan

No matter what your goal is behind reading this book, decide to make it your reality by creating a powerful plan of action. As Edwin Louis Cole, an American missionary, once said, "There are dreamers and there are planners; the planners make their dreams come true."

It is so very true as in the process of diligently following the plan, you have the potential to not only manifest what you desire but also to experience a profound transformation, fulfillment, and inspiration from a rebirth of a higher perception of life.

In the introduction, I asked you to rate seven aspects of your life from 1 to 10. How encouraging would it be to do this exercise one more time after expanding your knowledge and practicing the new skills given to you in this book?

Once again, write down on a piece of paper or in a notebook the seven areas of life and rate them from 1 to 10. This time, this exercise will guide you into creating an action plan. It will show you where your energy and attention should be directed. I will give you an example of this powerful exercise.

Below you can find random ratings for each area of life. Even though Heath and Prosperity belong to the same area, I separated them so that each aspect of it has an individual plan.

Prosperity	7
Health	3
Sexuality and Creativity	3
Confidence and Willpower	5
Love and Relationships	4
Communication Skills	9
Intuitive Abilities	6
Higher Consciousness	5

MASTERING IMBALANCES

I am introducing you to this example to show you how the chart may look. Lower numbers indicate an imbalance in the specific area. Nevertheless, if all areas of life have low numbers, that indicates a proportionately low quality of being, which must be addressed.

I recommend focusing your attention on the areas with the lowest ratings while continuing to strengthen all the other aspects, just like a skillful musician checks and tunes their instrument with love and passion each time they play it.

A POWERFUL PLAN

In the random rating above, the area of *Prosperity* was rated 7. Even though the number is not very low, there is always a space for growth, as once you stop expanding, you begin shrinking. This area is your ability to feel free financially and, as a result, be able not only to live a comfortable and happy life but also to positively impact those around you. Plans for continuous improvement in this area may look like this:

A) Work on expanding your consciousness—think bigger.
B) Continue to transform limiting beliefs and strengthen positive ones.
C) Elevate your intention behind success.
D) Develop or improve your mission statement and educate yourself on the topic of marketing.
E) Discover or start living your purpose more passionately.
F) Add new more powerful images of your successful life in the vision book.
G) Learn or continue exploring how to manifest with your heart.
H) Take decisive and proactive actions toward your goal.

Health was rated 3. How can you reach a higher rating? Health is one of your most important assets. As you have learned in the chapter "Health Is Your Wealth," your level of prosperity, motivation, and overall well-being is influenced by your health. The plan for improvement in this vital area of life may look like this:

A) Begin incorporating healthier foods and supplements.
B) Discover and research your blood type and incorporate the necessary suggestions.
C) Find time to care for your body by deepening your connection with it and exercising regularly.
D) Continue mastering emotional well-being.
E) Ensure that you rest and rejuvenate on a consistent basis.
F) Continue transforming mental addictions or childhood associations and discover healthier alternatives.

Sexuality and Creativity in this example was rated 3. This is an area that certainly requires loving attention. As you have learned in the chapter "Sexuality Is Sacred, Not Sinful," this area is a pathway into the world of inspired creativity, health, emotional balance, and manifestation of your dreams. The steps to improve this area could be:

A) Shift the way you perceive sexuality from shame to sacredness.
B) Rewire your subconscious programming.
C) Explore the sacred practice of Tantra.
D) Continue to expand love toward yourself and your body.
E) Continue practicing present-moment awareness.
F) Put it all into practice. You were created to experience feelings and deep sensations. Embrace life and learn to gracefully accept one of the most vital parts of you, *sexuality*.

Confidence and Willpower was rated 5. A powerful self-image greatly influences your state of being and is an integral part of any achievement. Developing willpower enables you to build a strong and powerful personality and will assist you in accomplishing your objectives more effectively. The plan for improvement may look like this:

A) Discover the root cause of unwanted patterns and ways to transform them.
B) Work on shifting negative inner talk and limiting beliefs.
C) Affirm new healthy ways of being and set reminders to practice them daily.
D) Change your story in conversations with others, from self-diminishing to self-empowering.

E) Add a more powerful version of you to the vision book.
F) Change the perception of yourself.
G) Alter your approach—from force to power.

Love and Relationships was rated 4. This area includes the relationship with yourself as well as an intimate connection. Cultivating a harmonious relationship can be a wonderful source of joy, support, and inspiration. The relationship with oneself directly reflects the relationship with your partner. Furthermore, the ability to build a lasting connection frequently serves as a catalyst for personal transformation. The plan for improvement in this area may look like this:

A) Treat yourself as you would treat someone you love dearly.
B) Regularly focus on transforming limiting beliefs.
C) Learn and experience new ways to communicate.
D) Explore the influence of childhood traits on the way you perceive any other relationship.
E) Study the influence of hormones on the emotions of you and your partner. Incorporate new healthy habits.
F) Continue to practice taming your mind as it can be the major reason for conflicts and havoc.
G) Open your heart to love unconditionally and learn to become more empathetic.

Communication Skills was rated 9. The rating is high, yet there is always a space to grow, evolve, and become better. Excellent communication skills are the doorway to successful relationships and favorable negotiations in every area of life. The plan for improving this essential area may look like:

A) Continue to practice being a great listener.
B) Expand your compassionate and empathetic nature.

C) Explore different communication styles.
D) Practice speaking from your heart.
E) Acquire knowledge about the elements of emotions and begin practicing the skill.
F) Gain or expand an understanding of the characteristics of the brain, both right and left.
G) Carry on applying power, not force, while in conversations with others.

Intuitive Abilities was rated 6. Remember, when you are intuitively connected, it is just so much easier to make choices that truly serve you. For that reason, continuous improvement in this area is the key to a successful and fulfilled life. A plan of action for enhancing intuitive abilities may look like:

A) Begin asking questions and practice discovering the insights.
B) Learn to distinguish how you receive intuitive messages.
C) Familiarize yourself with a restful mind, or rather a mindless state, to deepen your connection with Infinite Intelligence.
D) Start exploring your dreams and their powerful guidance.
E) Practice intuition exercises.
F) Learn to use spiritual attributes.

Higher Consciousness was rated 5. As you have learned from the chapter "The Power of Being Present," this area reflects your ability to appreciate every moment as each one of them is special. When you detach yourself from the envisioned outcomes, there is so much more potential for them to be materialized as unnecessary worries no longer stand in the way while ultimate trust prevails. The plan to improve this vital area may look like this:

A) Practice deep breathing exercises to shift attention away from the mind.
B) Begin experiencing life from the sacred space of your heart, feeling unconditional love and appreciation.
C) Spend time connecting with nature.
D) Detach from expectations and strong points of view.
E) Learn to return to a childlike innocence.
F) Learn to surrender and feel unconditional gratitude.

Master Your Plan

While you are in the process of mastering the plan, I highly recommend rereading the chapters on your weakest areas and putting forth effort to transform them. Also, place your plan in a visible spot as a reminder for continuous growth. Lastly, keep on exploring new avenues for further self-development.

I believe that in order to see major changes, it is essential to put in consistent work, even if those steps are small. The weakest areas will surely require more work, and that is where most of your attention should be directed.

I would like to repeat that a skillful musician checks each string of the instrument before playing to ensure a harmonious sound. That is why I highly recommend paying attention even to the strongest areas to experience profound and everlasting growth and transformation.

As Brian Tracy, a self-development author, once said, "Continuous learning is the minimum requirement for success in any field." For this reason, in addition to the knowledge you learned in this book, I recommend that you expand on this foundation by studying different courses, books, or seminars. Trust your intuition to guide you further toward the journey of self-discovery and infinite AbunDance.

Notice Your Growth

It is easier sometimes to notice what is not working in your life, rather than areas where you have progressed. I once heard a story about a family with three sons. Every year they visited their distant relatives in a small town. At the time of each visit, the three sons were complimented on their growth, both physical and mental.

The parents, though, did not notice it to the same degree because they were concentrating on the challenges along the way. They spent so much time with their children that the changes were not noticeable to their everyday eyes.

The distant relatives, on the contrary, hadn't see the children for a long time, so their growth was apparent to them. This story is a great example of becoming aware of your own inner growth as what you concentrate upon and notice, you invite into your life.

Celebrate Your Wins

The more you praise and celebrate your life, the more there is in life to celebrate. With even the smallest success that you honor, you create more of it in your life. That's when you are more prone to notice miracles than hardships. At this point, you develop a new personality that is driven, passionate, and constantly growing because you are paying attention to the right things while your life's path continues to evolve.

Your life can be compared to a spiral. When you are going upward, you still have to inevitably go through the lower part to lift yourself even higher. That is exactly when many people start believing that no progress has been made, or everything is working against them.

Recognize that it is not true; especially if you have been making an honest attempt. In this case you are simply being prepared for a more expanded and advanced step. Therefore, remind yourself daily to feel grateful for whatever lesson and circumstance appears on your path and celebrate your achievements.

Negative Emotions

It is okay sometimes to experience negative emotions. It is part of being human. They are your teachers rather than something to resent and focus your energy on. The next time you experience low vibrational feelings, take a breath, and ask yourself, "Why am I feeling this way? Is it truly necessary?" Realize that being okay with feeling negative emotions is actually the fastest way to release that state.

So, instead of holding resentment, be grateful to the situations or people who bring out pessimistic reactions in you because they show you what you still need to work on. When you feel negative, it is so easy to blame your circumstances or other people. Instead, take full and complete responsibility for what you are manifesting.

Often, when you feel negative, it is easy to spread low vibrations around you. This can lead to future guilt or even affect the quality of your connections with certain people. In anger or pain, you may say things that are hurtful to others. That is why if tension or unease occurs in you, take a few deep breaths, have a bath, sit quietly listening to healing music for a few minutes, or do anything that can help you alter your state.

It is easier to go along with negative emotions and intensify them when you let your thoughts influence how you feel. Instead, take a deep breath and experience the unwavering love and gratitude for all the wonderful things in your life. Your perception will be altered once you choose to tune in to this powerful state.

A BOOK OF YOUR DESTINY

In the chapter "Beyond Surviving—How to Thrive," I recommended you create a vision book. Now is the time to turn it into the book of your destiny by putting images of you being successful and content in every area of life. Those images should portray your envisioned dream life and resemble the ideal version of you. You can find them online, or in magazines.

For example, in the area of health and prosperity, you can place a picture of a perfectly shaped body; healthy foods and supplements; photos of your ideal home, car, vacations, or any other material accomplishments; and whatever else wellness and prosperity mean to you.

In the area of sexuality, you can add images of romance and a divine loving passionate connection. In the area of self-image, you can place a photo of your most confident and powerful self. In the area of love and relationships, add an image of a loving family happily enjoying every moment of life, or whatever else this area means for you.

In the area of communication skills, place a picture that represents you as an excellent communicator. It could be a picture of a deal you closed or of you successfully resolving a conflict.

In the area of intuitive abilities, add an image of you being connected with your intuitive guidance. It can be a spiritual picture of a third eye chakra, or you can draw purple rays that flow into you. It may also indicate anything else you believe is related to having a deep sense of intuition.

In the area of higher consciousness, you can add photos of nature to remember to be serene, and enough. You can put pictures of meditation or any other images that remind you to be present and to experience life from a higher state of consciousness.

Look at those images as often as possible and envision them as being already a part of your reality. Experience them fully in your heart and your body. When you begin living your life from this new vision, you begin manifesting it in the physical realm. Keep in mind to not limit yourself to what you can create, so leave space for possibilities.

Reminders

Without proper practice, it is very easy to revert to less beneficial or even destructive ways of experiencing life. That is when reminders become your greatest tool. They assist you in imprinting fresh, positive ways of being into your subconscious.

Put positive affirmations or images portraying mastery in the places where you will see them often. They will remind you where your energy and attention should flow. Also, don't forget it is not only about actions. Surrender and detachment toward the outcomes also play a big role in the manifestation of your visions as well.

Gratitude

Remember to feel gratitude. When you appreciate even small things, there will be more to feel grateful for, I promise. The feeling of gratitude will not only help you feel magnificent but also assist you in manifesting your visions as it places you in a frequency of complete trust in the universe.

In other words, by expressing appreciation, you stop doubting the journey and begin living your vision in the now. The Bible states it clearly: "Whatever you ask for in prayer, believe that you have received it, and it will be yours." *Mark 11:24*

So, write on your mirror or add a photo on the phone screen of the word "gratitude" to support your ongoing sense of appreciation. Everything in your reality will change as a result.

Recognize, when you feel grateful, you feel enough. When you feel enough, you are already successful. And the rest will be there in the right time, space, and sequence. Every part of the journey is preparing you for the next step. The more grateful you are for this part of it, the more effortlessly the doors of opportunities will start opening up.

Trust the process and allow miracles to unfold!